A
Scottish Ballad Book

The Scottish Series

General editor: Alexander Scott

The Scottish Series will include in its range books on every aspect of Scottish literature and social history from the earliest times to the present, including anthologies (both poetry and prose), new editions of Scottish classics, scholarly studies, critical surveys, and collections of essays. These volumes will be designed for the general reader and the serious student alike, and the editors of the various volumes will be recognised authorities in their different fields.

The first publication, in 1972, was *The Hugh MacDiarmid Anthology*, edited by Michael Grieve (MacDiarmid's son) and Alexander Scott. Issued in honour of the poet's eightieth birthday, it constituted the most representative selection of his work published to date, illustrating the full scope of Scotland's greatest living writer.

In addition to *A Scottish Ballad Book*, edited by David Buchan, Senior Lecturer in English Studies, University of Stirling, the following volumes are planned for publication:
Burns: Critical Essays, edited by Donald Low, Lecturer in English Studies, University of Stirling.

The 18th Century Scottish Lyric, edited by Thomas Crawford, Senior Lecturer in English, University of Aberdeen.

The general editor of the series, Alexander Scott—the poet, dramatist, critic and biographer—is Head of the Department of Scottish Literature in the University of Glasgow.

The Scottish Series

A
Scottish Ballad Book

Edited by
David Buchan

Routledge & Kegan Paul
London and Boston

*First published in 1973
by Routledge & Kegan Paul Ltd
Broadway House, 68-74 Carter Lane,
London EC4V 5EL and
9 Park Street,
Boston, 02108, U.S.A.*

*Printed in Great Britain by
T. & A. Constable Ltd
Hopetoun Street, Edinburgh
© this selection and arrangement,
introduction, notes, glossary: David Buchan 1973*

ISBN 0 7100 7566 9

821.008

SCO

To J. D. B. and E. A. B.

Now I'm for no idle lairdies; every man has to work, if it's only at peddling ballants; to work or to be wheeped; or to be haangit. (Hermiston in R. L. Stevenson, *Weir of Hermiston*).

Contents

Acknowledgments   xi

Introduction   1

The Oral Tradition

1. Gil Brenton   11
2. Willie's Lady   15
3. The Twa Sisters   18
4. King Henry   20
5. Allison Gross   23
6. Thomas Rymer   24
7. Young Bicham   26
8. Young Bekie   29
9. Fair Annie   33
10. Child Waters   36
11. Lady Maisry   40
12. The Lass of Roch Royal   44
13. Love Gregor   47
14. Fause Foodrage   51
15. Fair Mary of Wallington   55
16. Lamkin   56
17. The Gay Goshawk   59
18. Brown Robin   62
19. Johnie Scot   65
20. Willie o Douglas Dale   69
21. Rose the Red and White Lily   73

22. Sir Hugh   80

23. The Baron of Brackley   82

24. Bonny Baby Livingston   83

25. The Kitchie-Boy   88

The Tradition in Transition

26. Kemp Owyne   95

27. Tam Lin   97

28. Hind Etin   101

29. Lady Maisry   102

30. Lord Ingram and Chiel Wyet   106

31. The Clerk's Twa Sons o Owsenford   109

32. The Knight and Shepherd's Daughter   111

33. Mary Hamilton   118

34. Archie o Cawfield   120

35. The Fire of Frendraught   122

36. Bonny John Seton   125

37. Eppie Morrie   127

38. The Earl of Errol   129

39. Young Bearwell   131

40. The Young Laird of Craigstoun   133

The Modern Tradition (i)

41. The Elfin Knight   137

42. Lady Isabel and the Elf-Knight   138

43. Leesome Brand   140

44. Hind Horn   143

45. Bonnie Annie   146

Contents

46. Kempy Kay   146

47. The Twa Magicians   147

48. Captain Wedderburn's Courtship   148

49. Proud Lady Margaret   151

50. Sir Patrick Spens   152

51. Robin Hood and Allen a Dale   154

52. The Death of Queen Jane   156

53. Edom o Gordon   157

54. Edom o Gordon   158

55. The Gardener   159

56. The Duke of Gordon's Daughter   161

57. The Rantin Laddie   165

58. Young Allan   166

59. Lang Johnny More   169

60. The White Fisher   174

61. Our Goodman   177

62. Get Up and Bar the Door   180

63. The Wife Wrapt in Wether's Skin   181

The Modern Tradition (ii)

64. The Hireman Chiel   185

65. The Barnyards o Delgaty   191

66. Drumdelgie   192

67. John Bruce o the Forenit   194

68. Swaggers   196

69. Johnnie Sangster   198

70. Harrowing Time   200

Contents

71. The Tarves Rant   202

72. M'Ginty's Meal-an-Ale   204

     Tunes   207

     Notes   221

     Glossary   225

     Index   231

Acknowledgments

For permission to print material, my thanks are due to the University of Aberdeen, for texts and tunes from the Greig MSS., to the Buchan Club and the University of Aberdeen, for texts from *Last Leaves*, to the curator, Broughton House, Kirkcudbright, for a text from the Kirkpatrick Sharpe MSS., to Harvard College Library for tunes from the Ritson-Tytler Brown MS., and to Professor Bertrand Bronson and Princeton University Press for his transcriptions of these tunes in *The Traditional Tunes of the Child Ballads*.

Introduction

As the ballads have always exercised a wide-ranging appeal it may not be unduly utopian to declare that this ballad book is designed for both the general reader and the more academic student. For the reader who 'reads for enjoyment' there is here a fresh choosing of ballads, unencumbered by marginalia. For the ballad student who wishes to scrutinise this maverick of literary forms the texts are selected so that they can be examined in various perspectives.

In the first place, the material is selected from one regional tradition, that of the Northeast of Scotland, and for the most part from three tradition-bearers of that region. The material has been so chosen in the belief that ballads can be most rewardingly considered when located in place and time. In the past mystical notions about 'the folk' have severely hampered ballad studies, and indeed other areas of Folklife Studies; it is now a truism of Folklife Studies that folk literature texts should be seen not in the context of a vague mystical 'Volk', but in the context of a specific regional or group culture: hence the individual ballad tradition. As with place, so with time; the ballads are most helpfully seen not in terms of a misty undefined 'past age' but, at the very least, in the context of the period when the ballad-texts were recorded: hence the three tradition-bearers, whose texts were recorded in three different centuries – eighteenth, nineteenth and twentieth. As, moreover, a tradition comprises individual singers or reciters, it makes good sense to begin a study of a tradition with the study of the individuals' repertoires.

Why, then, the regional tradition of the Northeast of Scotland? The reasons are dealt with at some length in *The Ballad and the Folk* (Routledge & Kegan Paul, 1972), a book to which this anthology is complementary. Briefly, the Northeast provides a balladry unmatched in quality and quantity by any other regional culture in Britain. The Northeast's is also the only regional tradition where one can see clearly the three evolutionary stages of a ballad tradition: from oral to transitional to modern. The corpora of the three tradition-bearers – Anna Brown, James Nicol, Bell Robertson – represent these three stages, and in that of Anna Brown the Northeast tradition has the only sizeable corpus known to date of undoubtedly oral ballads.

That statement raises inevitably the thorny and basic question, 'What is a ballad?' The short reply – 'It is a narrative song that has been transmitted by tradition' – is not entirely satisfactory, as the processes of tradition have varied in response to social change. A longer, more satisfying, but more complicated account of the ballad has to take into consideration, first, ballad transmission, second, ballad-story, and third, ballad-text. General readers may prefer at this point to begin browsing in the lusher pastures of 'Gil Brenton'.

The three stages of tradition correspond to a culture's periods of nonliteracy, initial literacy, and settled literacy. It is the degree or outright absence of literacy that determines the kind of composition and transmission employed by the folk at different times. The folk of the oral tradition were nonliterate and it is their method of composition and transmission that has given the distinguishing traits to what we normally think of as 'the' ballads. Nonliterate people did not compose ballads as literate people compose poems, because the conditions of transmission differ appreciably in nonliterate and literate societies. In the latter, poems are transmitted visually, in print; in the former, ballads were transmitted aurally, from person to person. For the nonliterate singer the process necessitated his storing the material in the mind so that he could reproduce the stories readily in performance. The literate person, conditioned by the ways of his literate culture, will assume that the obvious method for dealing with this problem is rote memorisation of the heard text. Such, however, was not the way of the nonliterate singer. He learned both ballad-stories and a method of ballad composition, and in performance re-created the ballad-story by this method of composition to produce a ballad-text. Each performance, then, resulted in a freshly composed ballad-text.

This Introduction is hardly an appropriate place for discussing in detail the method of oral composition, and a brief account will necessarily involve a degree of over-simplification, but simply and crudely: the oral maker controls his material by patternings. For easy mental storage he reduces a heard ballad-story to its bare narrative essence, and then, in the act of composition, expands the nuclear story into a full-blown ballad-text through structural and formulaic patternings. These structural patternings enable him both to advance the story's episodes dramatically and to control proportionately the individual episodes in their relationship to each other and to the story as a whole. The formulaic patternings operate somewhat differently. Whatever poetic and melodic form the maker uses, whether quatrain or couplet, he must employ units of language which fit the metric, syntactic, and rhyming patterns of that form. In response to these limitations tradition evolves a restricted language, a kind of *Kunstsprache*, drawn from the spoken language, whose units do fit these patterns. The most frequently repeated units are the formulas – 'He hadna gane a mile, a mile', 'O saddle me the black, the black' and so on – but because all the units must meet the restrictions of the form, all the units of this *Kunstsprache* are formulaically patterned. And nowhere is the formulaic patterning more evident than in the rhyming, where a few sounds and a few words do most of the work. We literates with our stress on verbal creation may tend to emphasise the formulas in the method of composition, but it is arguable that for the nonliterate person the structuring bulked larger in importance. Certainly, from an analytic standpoint, it seems probable that the structuring provides a surer guide to the oral composition of a text than the formulas. The oral maker, then, relies when composing his text on the structural and formulaic patternings he inherits from tradition; and these are exemplified in the texts of Mrs Brown.

In a nonliterate society composing is a re-creative process in which the means of composition cannot be dissociated from the means of transmission. In a settled literate society composition and transmission become separate operations because with literacy comes the concept of the fixed text: the belief that a story *is* the words in which it is told rather than a platonic narrative essence capable of being concretely realised in variable words. Literacy takes away from the composer the pressures under which the oral poet creates and which have fashioned his medium; he can now compose in conditions of comparative leisure, draw thereby on much wider resources of language, and produce a visible text. This text is *the* poem, not one re-creation in a chain of re-creations; the poem has become a fixed text. In modern tradition not only are the new poems composed differently but the old poems are also transmitted differently, because people come to believe that they too must have a fixed text. Consequently the singers and reciters of modern tradition memorise the 'right' text of an old ballad-story, which may be one seen in print, or heard from another singer or from some modern mechanical medium. Whereas in oral tradition composition and transmission were both part of the same re-creative, self-renewing process, in modern tradition composition is one distinct activity and transmission another, but basically noncreative, activity. Naturally a regional tradition does not pass from oral to modern overnight; it goes through a period of transition when the local culture is adjusting to the spread of literacy. In this situation singers adopt to their stories a loosely re-creative attitude. They do not compose in the fully re-creative oral-traditional manner – in which case their recorded texts would be oral texts, which they are not – nor do they merely memorise in the modern-traditional manner – in which case the texts would again be (slightly chipped) oral texts. They are re-creative in that they are as yet unburdened by notions of the fixed text; but they are loosely re-creative in that they do not compose their texts through the strict disciplines of the old structural and formulaic patternings. Nicol's ballad-texts exemplify the transitional mode and Bell Robertson's the modern mode of transmission.

Just as there are three kinds of transmission there are three kinds of ballad-story found in tradition: oral, chap, and modern. Oral ballad-stories are narratives composed and re-composed by a traditional oral method; chap ballad-stories are narratives composed or re-worked in subliterary style by commercial entrepreneurs expressly for traditional singers; and modern ballad-stories are non-commercial narratives composed in subliterary style normally by singers within the tradition. In general, the three kinds correspond to the three stages of a tradition's development.

So far, we have considered the three kinds of ballad transmission and the three kinds of ballad-story; when correlated, they provide us with the various kinds of ballad-text. The oral ballad-story produces, by oral transmission, oral texts; by transitional transmission, oral-transitional texts; and by modern transmission, memorised reproductions of oral and oral-transitional texts. The chap ballad-story appears initially in a printed text, and then produces, by transitional transmission, chap-transitional texts, and by modern transmission, memorised reproductions of printed and chap-transitional texts. The modern ballad-story appears initially in a written or printed text, or even a record, and then produces, by modern transmission, memorised reproductions of this modern text.

As the oral ballads make up the backbone of tradition, besides being the most interesting artistically of traditional narrative songs, most of the texts that follow are versions of oral ballad-stories. All the Anna Brown ballads are oral texts. All the James Nicol ballads are oral-transitional texts, although his 'Kemp Owyne' comes very close to being oral. The Bell Robertson selection contains modern reproductions of oral texts in 'Leesome Brand' and 'Hind Horn', but is made up for the most part of reproductions of oral-transitional texts. It also includes some chap-transitional texts. Her version of 'The Duke of Gordon's Daughter' derives from a story composed along fairly traditional lines by the chap industry that became one of the favourite broadside ballads of the Northeast. On the other hand, her chap-transitional texts of 'Lady Isabel and the Elf-Knight', 'The Gardener', and 'The Rantin Laddie' derive from chapbook or broadside reworkings of traditional stories; while 'Our Goodman' derives from a book text and 'Proud Lady Margaret' has two stanzas from the book text of a different ballad. The final section of the bothy ballads contains modern ballad-stories in modern texts.

Narratively the ballads are chosen both to represent the varieties of stories found in the regional tradition and to exemplify the major categories of ballad subject-matter: magical and marvellous ballads, romantic and tragic ballads, historical and semi-historical ballads. The largest single group is that of the romantic and tragic ballads: 7, 9, 10, 11, 12, 13, 14, 15, 16, 17, 18, 19, 20, 21, 25, 29, 30, 31, 32, 39, 48, 55, 58, 60. Most deal with the happy uniting or unhappy sundering of a pair of lovers; the former generally concentrate on the brave or resourceful overcoming of the obstacles to the union, and the latter generally concentrate on the events that lead up to the death of hero or heroine as a result of a relative's implacable hostility. 'Fause Foodrage' and 'Lamkin' have murder and revenge as their theme, while 'Young Allan' is one of the few sea-adventure stories.

The magical and marvellous ballads are 1, 2, 3, 4, 5, 6, 8, 26, 27, 28, 41, 42, 43, 44, 45, 47, 49. These stories are shaped by folk belief and suffused with lore of the Otherworld and witchcraft lore. They are populated by elf-knights, ladies bespelled into hags, monsters, revenants, witches, fairy queens and hosts and their human captives, magicians, and helpful spirits like the Belly Blin. They have as crucial elements in the narrative a miraculous rebirth or harps and rings with magical properties or, as in 'Bonnie Annie' (and 'Young Allan'), ships with a responsive intelligence. As the reference to 'Young Allan' indicates, these two groups – like all the groups – tend to overlap. That these groupings can only be approximate is particularly evident when one considers together 'Hind Horn', 'Young Bicham', 'Young Bekie', and 'The Kitchie-Boy', for they are all variations on the same 'return after long absence' theme that is found throughout oral tradition and most spectacularly in the *Odyssey*.

The historical and semi-historical ballads are 22, 23, 24, 33, 34, 35, 36, 37, 38, 40, 50, 51, 52, 53, 54, 56, 57. 'Robin Hood and Allen a Dale' and 'Sir Hugh' deal with legendary figures and events of ostensible English origin. 'Sir Patrick Spens' grows out of incidents in Scottish-Scandinavian political history. 'The Death of Queen Jane' and 'Mary Hamilton' take place at the courts of England and Scotland respectively, and 'Archie o Cawfield' is a sturdy representative of the riding ballads from the Scottish–English border. 'Edom o Gordon', 'The Fire of Frendraught', 'Bonny John Seton', and 'The Baron of

Brackley' derive from Northeast feuds, which are often regional expressions of national political tensions. 'Bonny Baby Livingston' and 'Eppie Morrie' may not relate actual happenings but do reflect the pattern of events along the Northeast's Highland/Lowland border; bride-stealing seems to have been a ubiquitous feature of life in European ballad communities. The remaining three are all anecdotes about local lairds: 'The Earl of Errol' has a basis in fact, and 'The Young Laird of Craigstoun' may have a basis in fact in the story of John Urquhart and Elizabeth Innes, but 'The Rantin Laddie' has no ascertainable basis in fact.

In addition to the major groups, there is a small group of comic ballads: 46, 59, 61, 62, 63. 'Our Goodman', 'Get Up and Bar the Door', and 'The Wife Wrapt in Wether's Skin' rely on comedy of situation and incident while 'Kempy Kay' and 'Lang Johnny More' go in for the comedy of broad exaggeration. Both in fact have elements of parody, on the one hand, of the chivalric unspelling of the loathly hag into beautiful woman, and on the other, of the heroic rescue from jail story. Some minor sub-groups that fall within larger groups have their representatives. The riddling ballads are exemplified by 'The Elfin Knight' and 'Captain Wedderburn's Courtship', and the ballads of yeoman minstrelsy (to use M. J. C. Hodgart's description) by 'Robin Hood and Allen a Dale'. The ballads typified by the long Arthurian stories in the Percy MS. and called by Hodgart the ballads of late medieval minstrelsy* do not seem to have been a Scottish phenomenon, but some of the ballad-texts collected by Peter Buchan and printed at the very end of Child's collection may be the descendants of Scottish equivalents, since they do have links, though sometimes rather tenuous, with stories of the romances. The representative of this category is 'Young Bearwell', an incomplete piece which nevertheless has some motifs in common with the romance 'King Horn'.

The bothy ballads chosen represent the main concerns of their kind. They deal with the work at specific farms, aspects of the labour and leisure, and humorous incidents of farm life. Introducing them is a song which links them to the older minstrelsy, and rounding them off is a song by a highly individual composer in the genre, George Bruce Thomson, which points forward to the Scottish music-hall. Artistically these songs do not stand comparison with the older ballads, but their great virtue is that they tell honestly and accurately what the hard but frequently humoursome bothy life was like. Although the bothy

---

* *The Ballads*, 2nd ed., London, 1962, p. 14.

ballads make up the most characteristic element of the modern regional tradition, they are very far from constituting the whole; for the full variety of narrative song in the modern tradition we must await the edition, now under way, of the Greig and Duncan MSS.

The ballads, it has often been remarked, are more than stories, they are sung stories; but only one of our three tradition-bearers, Anna Brown, has left any music for her texts. No record exists of any tunes that Nicol may have sung to, while Bell Robertson did not sing at all. The Anna Brown tunes are printed according to the transcription by Professor Bertrand Bronson in *The Traditional Tunes of the Child Ballads* (Princeton, N.J., 1959–72), and the bothy ballad tunes have been copied from the Greig MSS. at the University of Aberdeen by Pat Shuldham-Shaw, the editor of the Greig and Duncan MSS.

Ballads differ from conventional poems not only because they are sung but also because they have been transmitted by word of mouth, by the oral tradition of nonliterate society and the verbal tradition of literate society, and hence belong to traditional culture (which may be defined as the culture transmitted by word of mouth and by custom and practice rather than by written or printed document). Traditional culture is the concern of Folklife Studies, and ballad study gains greatly from the perspective of this – for Britain relatively new – discipline, whose methodology is expressly designed for the problems presented by traditional material, and whose genres are interlinked in subject-matter. Throughout the ballads, for example, occur motifs found internationally in tradition and classified in one of the discipline's standard reference works – Stith Thompson's *Motif-Index of Folk Literature.** Balladry's most obvious correlations, however, are with the various kinds of folk narrative, though comparatively few ballads have precise counterparts in recorded folktales. Two ballads of this selection, the tragic 'Twa Sisters' and the comic 'Get Up and Bar the Door', appear in Märchen and Schwank form respectively as 'The Singing Bone' (A-T 780) and 'The Silence Wager' (A-T 1351).† A number, however, share themes and motifs with folktales as 'King

---

* 6 vols, Folklore Fellows Communications nos 106-9, 116, 117, Helsinki, 1932-6.
† A-T is the reference to the classification number in Antii Aarne and Stith Thompson, *The Types of the Folktale*, Folklore Fellows Communications no. 3, 2nd revision, Helsinki, 1961. These two stories have been studied in monographs: Lutz Mackensen, *Der singende Knochen*, FFC no. 49, Helsinki, 1923, and W. N. Brown, 'The Silence Wager Stories: their Origin and their Diffusion', *American Journal of Philology*, **43** (1922), 289-317.

Henry', 'Kemp Owyne', and 'Allison Gross' do with the stories numbered in Aarne-Thompson between 400 and 450. Some ballads link with other forms of folk narrative; 'Robin Hood and Allen a Dale' and 'Sir Hugh' may be seen in relation to legend, and the variant stories of 'Johnie Scot' and 'Lang Johnny More' may be seen as equivalents to hero tale and, one stage further from reality, tall tale. One of the verbal genres of Folklife Studies, the riddle, occurs in a number of ballads, as here in 'Captain Wedderburn's Courtship' where an exchange of riddles constitutes the dramatic action, but in general the ballads are remarkably lacking in proverbs and proverbial language. Elements of folk belief permeate many of the texts, though instances of folk custom appear more in hints and glimpses.

For the ballad student, then, this anthology has been designed to serve a number of functions: to provide a representative selection from one regional tradition, the tradition with the best of ballad-texts in the oral versions of Anna Brown and the widest range of ballad-stories; to exemplify the methods of composition and transmission, the kinds of ballad-story, and the kinds of ballad-text found in the oral, transitional, and modern stages of a ballad tradition; to exemplify the variety of ballad subject-matter; and to indicate some lines of relationship with the other genres of Folklife Studies. One other factor has operated on the selection. All anthologists try to maintain a balance between the familiar and the fresh, but in the case of the ballads what is familiar may not be representatively ballad-like. In choosing the texts I have tried to counteract the tendency of some literature anthologies to represent the ballads as 'narrative poetry' with a handful of short pieces, often largely lyric or all dialogue: the texts, in short, that come closest to a literate man's conception of simple, if arresting, poetry. As Anna Brown's often lengthy versions will show, the ballad is a narrative form of a distinct kind capable, within its own limits and on its own terms, of narrative complexity and sophistication.

The texts of Anna Brown's ballads are from the Brown MSS. via F. J. Child, *The English and Scottish Popular Ballads*, 5 vols, Boston, 1882-98. Nicol's texts – all bar one – come from a variety of sources via Child, the exception being 'The Young Laird of Craigstoun' which derives from Charles Kirkpatrick Sharpe's transcript of the 'North Country Ballads'. Two of Bell Robertson's texts derive from the Greig MSS., the remainder from the Greig MSS. via Gavin Greig, *Last Leaves of Traditional Ballads and Ballad Airs*, ed. Alex. Keith, Aberdeen, 1925. The bothy ballads are transcribed from the Greig MSS.

The Oral Tradition: The Ballads of Anna Brown

[Ch 5A]*   1. Gil Brenton

1   Gil Brenton has sent oer the fame,
       He's woo'd a wife an brought her hame.

2   Full sevenscore o ships came her wi,
       The lady by the greenwood tree.

3   There was twal an twal wi beer an wine,
       An twal an twal wi muskadine:

4   An twall an twall wi bouted flowr,
       An twall an twall wi paramour:

5   An twall an twall wi baken bread,
       An twall an twall wi the goud sae red.

6   Sweet Willy was a widow's son,
       An at her stirrup-foot he did run.

7   An she was dressd i the finest pa,
       But ay she loot the tears down fa.

8   An she was deckd wi the fairest flowrs,
       But ay she loot the tears down pour.

9   'O is there water i your shee?
       Or does the win blaw i your glee?

10   'Or are you mourning i your meed
       That eer you left your mither gueede?

11   'Or are ye mourning i your tide
       That ever ye was Gil Brenton's bride?'

12   'The[re] is nae water i my shee,
       Nor does the win blaw i my glee:

13   'Nor am I mourning i my tide
       That eer I was Gil Brenton's bride:

14   'But I am mourning i my meed
       That ever I left my mither gueede.

15   'But, bonny boy, tell to me
       What is the customs o your country.'

---

* This refers to the ballad-story number and ballad-text letter in Child.

'The customs o't, my dame,' he says,   16
'Will ill a gentle lady please.

'Seven king's daughters has our king wedded,   17
An seven king's daughters has our king bedded.

'But he's cutted the paps frae their breast-bane,   18
An sent them mourning hame again.

"But whan you come to the palace yate,   19
His mither a golden chair will set.

'An be you maid or be you nane,   20
O sit you there till the day be dane.

'An gin you're sure that you are a maid,   21
Ye may gang safely to his bed.

'But gin o that you be na sure,   22
Then hire some woman o youre bowr.'

O whan she came to the palace yate,   23
His mither a golden chair did set.

An was she maid or was she nane,   24
She sat in it till the day was dane.

An she's calld on her bowr woman,   25
That waiting was her bowr within.

'Five hundred pound, maid, I'll gi to the,   26
An sleep this night wi the king for me.'

Whan bells was rung, an mass was sung,   27
An a' man unto bed was gone,

Gil Brenton an the bonny maid   28
Intill ae chamber they were laid.

'O speak to me, blankets, an speak to me, sheets,   29
An speak to me, cods, that under me sleeps;

'Is this a maid that I ha wedded?   30
Is this a maid that I ha bedded?'

'It's nae a maid that you ha wedded,   31
But it's a maid that you ha bedded.

32   'Your lady's in her bigly bowr,
     An for you she drees mony sharp showr.'

33   O he has taen him thro the ha,
     And on his mither he did ca.

34   'I am the most unhappy man
     That ever was in christend lan.

35   'I woo'd a maiden meek an mild,
     An I've marryed a woman great wi child.'

36   'O stay, my son, intill this ha,
     An sport you wi your merry men a'.

37   'An I'll gang to yon painted bowr,
     An see how't fares wi yon base whore.'

38   The auld queen she was stark an strang;
     She gard the door flee aff the ban.

39   The auld queen she was stark an steer;
     She gard the door lye i the fleer.

40   'O is your bairn to laird or loon?
     Or is it to your father's groom?

41   'My bairn's na to laird or loon,
     Nor is it to my father's groom.

42   'But hear me, mither, on my knee,
     An my hard wierd I'll tell to thee.

43   'O we were sisters, sisters seven,
     We was the fairest under heaven.

44   'We had nae mair for our seven years wark
     But to shape an sue the king's son a sark.

45   'O it fell on a Saturday's afternoon,
     Whan a' our langsome wark was dane,

46   'We keist the cavils us amang,
     To see which shoud to the greenwood gang.

47   'Ohone, alas! for I was youngest,
     An ay my wierd it was the hardest.

'The cavil it did on me fa,   48
Which was the cause of a' my wae.

'For to the greenwood I must gae,   49
To pu the nut but an the slae;

'To pu the red rose an the thyme,   50
To strew my mother's bowr and mine.

'I had na pu'd a flowr but ane,   51
Till by there came a jelly hind greeme,

'Wi high-colld hose an laigh-colld shoone,   52
An he 'peard to be some kingis son.

'An be I maid or be I nane,   53
He kept me there till the day was dane.

'An be I maid or be I nae,   54
He kept me there till the close of day.

'He gae me a lock of yallow hair,   55
An bade me keep it for ever mair.

'He gae me a carket o gude black beads,   56
An bade me keep them against my needs.

'He gae to me a gay gold ring,   57
An bade me ke[e]p it aboon a' thing.

'He gae to me a little pen-kniffe,   58
An bade me keep it as my life.'

'What did you wi these tokens rare   59
That ye got frae that young man there?'

'O bring that coffer hear to me,   60
And a' the tokens ye sal see.'

An ay she rauked, an ay she flang,   61
Till a' the tokens came till her han.

'O stay here, daughter, your bowr within,   62
Till I gae parley wi my son.'

O she has taen her thro the ha,   63
An on her son began to ca.

64　　'What did you wi that gay gold ring
　　　I bade you keep aboon a' thing?

65　　'What did you wi that little pen-kniffe
　　　I bade you keep while you had life?

66　　'What did you wi that yallow hair
　　　I bade you keep for ever mair?

67　　'What did you wi that good black beeds
　　　I bade you keep against your needs?'

68　　'I gae them to a lady gay
　　　I met i the greenwood on a day.

69　　'An I would gi a' my father's lan,
　　　I had that lady my yates within.

70　　'I would gi a' my ha's an towrs,
　　　I had that bright burd i my bowrs.'

71　　'O son, keep still your father's lan;
　　　You hae that lady your yates within.

72　　'An keep you still your ha's an towrs;
　　　You hae that bright burd i your bowrs.'

73　　Now or a month was come an gone,
　　　This lady bare a bonny young son.

74　　An it was well written on his breast-bane
　　　'Gil Brenton is my father's name.'

[Ch 6]　　　2. Willie's Lady

1　　Willie has taen him oer the fame,
　　He's woo'd a wife and brought her hame.

2　　He's woo'd her for her yellow hair,
　　But his mother wrought her mickle care.

3　　And mickle dolour gard her dree,
　　For lighter she can never be.

But in her bower she sits wi pain,   4
And Willie mourns oer her in vain.

And to his mother he has gone,   5
That vile rank witch of vilest kind.

He says: 'My ladie has a cup,   6
Wi gowd and silver set about.

'This goodlie gift shall be your ain,   7
And let her be lighter o her young bairn.'

'Of her young bairn she'll neer be lighter,   8
Nor in her bower to shine the brighter.

'But she shall die and turn to clay,   9
And you shall wed another may.'

'Another may I'll never wed,   10
Another may I'll neer bring home.'

But sighing says that weary wight,   11
'I wish my life were at an end.'

'Ye doe [ye] unto your mother again,   12
That vile rank witch of vilest kind.

'And say your ladie has a steed,   13
The like o'm 's no in the lands of Leed.

'For he [i]s golden shod before,   14
And he [i]s golden shod behind.

'And at ilka tet of that horse's main,   15
There's a golden chess and a bell ringing.

'This goodlie gift shall be your ain,   16
And let me be lighter of my young bairn.'

'O her young bairn she'll neer be lighter,   17
Nor in her bower to shine the brighter.

'But she shall die and turn to clay,   18
And ye shall wed another may.'

'Another may I['ll] never wed,   19
Another may I['ll] neer bring hame.'

20   But sighing said that weary wight,
'I wish my life were at an end.'

21   'Ye doe [ye] unto your mother again,
That vile rank witch of vilest kind.

22   'And say your ladie has a girdle,
It's red gowd unto the middle.

23   'And ay at every silver hem,
Hangs fifty silver bells and ten.

24   'That goodlie gift has be her ain,
And let me be lighter of my young bairn.'

25   'O her young bairn she's neer be lighter,
Nor in her bower to shine the brighter.

26   'But she shall die and turn to clay,
And you shall wed another may.'

27   'Another may I'll never wed,
Another may I'll neer bring hame.'

28   But sighing says that weary wight,
'I wish my life were at an end.'

29   Then out and spake the Belly Blind;
He spake aye in good time.

30   'Ye doe ye to the market place,
And there ye buy a loaf o wax.

31   'Ye shape it bairn and bairnly like,
And in twa glassen een ye pit;

32   'And bid her come to your boy's christening;
Then notice weel what she shall do.

33   'And do you stand a little fore bye,
And listen weel what she shall say.'

34   'Oh wha has loosed the nine witch knots
That was amo that ladie's locks?

35   'And wha has taen out the kaims of care
That hangs amo that ladie's hair?

'And wha's taen down the bush o woodbine   36
That hang atween her bower and mine?

'And wha has killd the master kid   37
That ran beneath that ladie's bed?

'And wha has loosed her left-foot shee,   38
And lotten that ladie lighter be?'

O Willie has loosed the nine witch knots   39
That was amo that ladie's locks

And Willie's taen out the kaims o care   40
That hang amo that ladie's hair.

And Willie's taen down the bush o woodbine   41
That hang atween her bower and thine.

And Willie has killed the master kid   42
That ran beneath that ladie's bed.

And Willie has loosed her left-foot shee,   43
And letten his ladie lighter be.

And now he's gotten a bonny young son,   44
And mickle grace be him upon.

3. The Twa Sisters   [*Ch 10B*]

There was twa sisters in a bowr,   1
   Edinburgh, Edinburgh
There was twa sisters in a bowr,
   Stirling for ay
There was twa sisters in a bowr,
There came a knight to be their wooer.
   Bonny Saint Johnston stands upon Tay.

He courted the eldest wi glove an ring,   2
But he lovd the youngest above a' thing.

He courted the eldest wi brotch an knife,   3
But lovd the youngest as his life.

4   The eldest she was vexed sair,
         An much envi'd her sister fair.

5   Into her bowr she could not rest,
         Wi grief an spite she almos brast.

6   Upon a morning fair an clear,
         She cried upon her sister dear:

7   'O sister, come to yon sea stran,
         An see our father's ships come to lan.'

8   She's taen her by the milk-white han,
         An led her down to yon sea stran.

9   The younges[t] stood upon a stane,
         The eldest came an threw her in.

10   She tooke her by the middle sma,
         An dashd her bonny back to the jaw.

11   'O sister, sister, tak my han,
         An Ise mack you heir to a' my lan.

12   'O sister, sister, tak my middle,
         An yes get my goud and my gouden girdle.

13   'O sister, sister, save my life,
         An I swear Ise never be nae man's wife.'

14   'Foul fa the han that I should tacke,
         It twin'd me an my wardles make.

15   'Your cherry cheeks an yallow hair
         Gars me gae maiden for evermair.'

16   Sometimes she sank, an sometimes she swam,
         Till she came down yon bonny mill-dam.

17   O out it came the miller's son,
         An saw the fair maid swimmin in.

18   'O father, father, draw your dam,
         Here's either a mermaid or a swan.'

19   The miller quickly drew the dam,
         An there he found a drownd woman.

You coudna see her yallow hair   20
For gold and pearle that were so rare.

You coudna see her middle sma   21
For gouden girdle that was sae braw.

You coudna see her fingers white,   22
For gouden rings that was sae gryte.

An by there came a harper fine,   23
That harped to the king at dine.

When he did look that lady upon,   24
He sighd and made a heavy moan.

He's taen three locks o her yallow hair,   25
An wi them strung his harp sae fair.

The first tune he did play and sing,   26
Was, 'Farewell to my father the king.'

The nextin tune that he playd syne,   27
Was, 'Farewell to my mother the queen.'

The lasten tune that he playd then,   28
Was, 'Wae to my sister, fair Ellen.'

4. King Henry [Ch 32]

Lat never a man a wooing wend   I
    That lacketh thingis three;
A routh o gold, an open heart,
    Ay fu o charity.

As this I speak of King Henry,   2
    For he lay burd-alone;
An he's doen him to a jelly hunt's ha,
    Was seven miles frae a town.

He chas'd the deer now him before,   3
    An the roe down by the den,
Till the fattest buck in a' the flock
    King Henry he has slain.

4   O he has doen him to his ha,
            To make him beerly cheer;
        An in it came a griesly ghost,
            Steed stappin i the fleer.

5   Her head hat the reef-tree o the house,
            Her middle ye mot wel span;
        He's thrown to her his gay mantle,
            Says, 'Lady, hap your lingcan.'

6   Her teeth was a' like teather stakes,
            Her nose like club or mell;
        An I ken naething she 'peard to be,
            But the fiend that wons in hell.

7   'Some meat, some meat, ye King Henry,
            Some meat ye gie to me!'
        'An what meat's in this house, lady,
            An what ha I to gie?'
        'O ye do kill your berry-brown steed,
            An you bring him here to me.'

8   O whan he slew his berry-brown steed,
            Wow but his heart was sair!
        Shee eat him [a'] up, skin an bane,
            Left naething but hide an hair.

9   'Mair meat, mair meat, ye King Henry,
            Mair meat ye gi to me!'
        'An what meat's in this house, lady,
            An what ha I to gi?'
        'O ye do kill your good gray-hounds,
            An ye bring them a' to me.'

10   O whan he slew his good gray-hounds,
            Wow but his heart was sair!
        She eat them a' up, skin an bane,
            Left naething but hide an hair.

11   'Mair meat, mair meat, ye King Henry,
            Mair meat ye gi to me!'
        'An what meat's i this house, lady,
            An what ha I to gi?'
        'O ye do kill your gay gos-hawks,
            An ye bring them here to me.'

O whan he slew his gay gos-hawks, 12
    Wow but his heart was sair!
She eat them a' up, skin an bane,
    Left naething but feathers bare.

'Some drink, some drink, now, King Henry, 13
    Some drink ye bring to me!'
'O what drink's i this house, lady,
    That you're nae welcome ti?'
'O ye sew up your horse's hide,
    An bring in a drink to me.'

And he's sewd up the bloody hide, 14
    A puncheon o wine put in;
She drank it a' up at a waught,
    Left na ae drap ahin.

'A bed, a bed, now, King Henry, 15
    A bed you mak to me!
For ye maun pu the heather green,
    An mak a bed to me.'

O pu'd has he the heather green, 16
    An made to her a bed,
An up has he taen his gay mantle,
    An oer it has he spread.

'Tak off your claiths, now, King Henry, 17
    An lye down by my side!'
'O God forbid,' says King Henry,
    'That ever the like betide;
That ever the fiend that wons in hell
    Shoud streak down by my side.'

*   *   *

Whan night was gane, and day was come, 18
    An the sun shone throw the ha,
The fairest lady that ever was seen
    Lay atween him an the wa.

'O well is me!' says King Henry, 19
    'How lang'll this last wi me?'
Then out it spake that fair lady,
    'Even till the day you dee.

20   'For I've met wi mony a gentle knight
            That's gien me sic a fill,
        But never before wi a courteous knight
            That ga me a' my will.'

[*Ch 35*]   5. Allison Gross

1   O Allison Gross, that lives in yon towr,
            The ugliest witch i the north country,
        Has trysted me ae day up till her bowr,
            An monny fair speech she made to me.

2   She stroaked my head, an she kembed my hair,
            An she set me down saftly on her knee;
        Says, Gin ye will be my lemman so true,
            Sae monny braw things as I woud you gi.

3   She showd me a mantle o red scarlet,
            Wi gouden flowrs an fringes fine;
        Says, Gin ye will be my lemman so true,
            This goodly gift it sal be thine.

4   'Awa, awa, ye ugly witch,
            Haud far awa, an lat me be;
        I never will be your lemman sae true,
            An I wish I were out o your company.'

5   She neist brought a sark o the saftest silk,
            Well wrought wi pearles about the ban;
        Says, Gin you will be my ain true love,
            This goodly gift you sal comman.

6   She showd me a cup of the good red gold,
            Well set wi jewls sae fair to see;
        Says, Gin you will be my lemman sae true,
            This goodly gift I will you gi.

7   'Awa, awa, ye ugly witch,
            Had far awa, and lat me be;
        For I woudna ance kiss your ugly mouth
            For a' the gifts that ye coud gi.'

She's turnd her right and roun about,　　　　8
　　An thrice she blaw on a grass-green horn,
An she sware by the meen and the stars abeen,
　　That she'd gar me rue the day I was born.

Then out has she taen a silver wand,　　　　9
　　An she's turnd her three times roun and roun;
She's muttered sich words till my strength it faild,
　　An I fell down senceless upon the groun.

She's turnd me into an ugly worm,　　　　10
　　And gard me toddle about the tree;
An ay, on ilka Saturdays night,
　　My sister Maisry came to me,

Wi silver bason an silver kemb,　　　　11
　　To kemb my heady upon her knee;
But or I had kissd her ugly mouth,
　　I'd rather a toddled about the tree.

But as it fell out on last Hallow-even,　　　　12
　　When the seely court was ridin by,
The queen lighted down on a gowany bank,
　　Nae far frae the tree where I wont to lye.

She took me up in her milk-white han,　　　　13
　　An she's stroakd me three times oer her knee;
She chang'd me again to my ain proper shape,
　　An I nae mair maun toddle about the tree.

6. Thomas Rymer　　[*Ch 37A*]

True Thomas lay oer yond grassy bank,　　　　1
　　And he beheld a ladie gay,
A ladie that was brisk and bold,
　　Come riding oer the fernie brae.

Her skirt was of the grass-green silk,　　　　2
　　Her mantel of the velvet fine,
At ilka tett of her horse's mane
　　Hung fifty silver bells and nine.

3   True Thomas he took off his hat,
         And bowed him low down till his knee:
     'All hail, thou mighty Queen of Heaven!
         For your peer on earth I never did see.'

4   'O no, O no, True Thomas,' she says,
         'That name does not belong to me;
     I am but the queen of fair Elfland,
         And I'm come here for to visit thee.

                    *   *   *

5   'But ye maun go wi me now, Thomas,
         True Thomas, ye maun go wi me,
     For ye maun serve me seven years,
         Thro weel or wae as may chance to be.'

6   She turned about her milk-white steed,
         And took True Thomas up behind,
     And aye wheneer her bridle rang,
         The steed flew swifter than the wind.

7   O they rade on, and further on,
         Until they came to a garden green:
     'Light down, light down, ye ladie free,
         Some of that fruit let me pull to thee.'

8   'O no, O no, True Thomas,' she says,
         'That fruit maun not be touched by thee,
     For a' the plagues that are in hell
         Light on the fruit of this countrie.

9   'But I have a loaf here in my lap,
         Likewise a bottle of claret wine,
     And now ere we go farther on,
         We'll rest a while, and ye may dine.'

10   When he had eaten and drunk his fill,
         'Lay down your head upon my knee,'
     The lady sayd, 'ere we climb yon hill,
         And I will show you fairlies three.

11   'O see not ye yon narrow road,
         So thick beset wi thorns and briers?
     That is the path of righteousness,
         Tho after it but few enquires.

'And see not ye that braid braid road,   12
   That lies across yon lillie leven?
That is the path of wickedness,
   Tho some call it the road to heaven.

'And see not ye that bonny road,   13
   Which winds about the fernie brae?
That is the road to fair Elfland,
   Whe[re] you and I this night maun gae.

'But Thomas, ye maun hold your tongue,   14
   Whatever you may hear or see,
For gin ae word you should chance to speak,
   You will neer get back to your ain countrie.'

For forty days and forty nights   15
   He wade thro red blude to the knee,
And he saw neither sun nor moon,
   But heard the roaring of the sea.

He has gotten a coat of the even cloth,   16
   And a pair of shoes of velvet green,
And till seven years were past and gone
   True Thomas on earth was never seen.

7. Young Bicham [Ch 53A]
(Young Beichan)

In London city was Bicham born,   1
   He longd strange countries for to see,
But he was taen by a savage Moor,
   Who handld him right cruely.

For thro his shoulder he put a bore,   2
   An thro the bore has pitten a tree,
An he's gard him draw the carts o wine,
   Where horse and oxen had wont to be.

He's casten [him] in a dungeon deep,   3
   Where he coud neither hear nor see;
He's shut him up in a prison strong,
   An he's handld him right cruely.

4 O this Moor he had but ae daughter,
    I wot her name was Shusy Pye;
  She's doen her to the prison-house,
    And she's called Young Bicham one word by.

5 'O hae ye ony lands or rents,
    Or citys in your ain country,
  Coud free you out of prison strong,
    An coud mantain a lady free?'

6 'O London city is my own,
    An other citys twa or three,
  Coud loose me out o prison strong,
    An coud mantain a lady free.'

7 O she has bribed her father's men
    Wi meikle goud and white money,
  She's gotten the key o the prison doors,
    An she has set Young Bicham free.

8 She's gi'n him a loaf o good white bread,
    But an a flask o Spanish wine,
  An she bad him mind on the ladie's love
    That sae kindly freed him out o pine.

9 'Go set your foot on good ship-board,
    An haste you back to your ain country,
  An before that seven years has an end,
    Come back again, love, and marry me.'

10 It was long or seven years had an end
    She longd fu sair her love to see;
  She's set her foot on good ship-board,
    An turned her back on her ain country.

11 She's saild up, so has she doun,
    Till she came to the other side;
  She's landed at Young Bicham's gates,
    An I hop this day she sal be his bride.

12 'Is this Young Bicham's gates?' says she,
    'Or is that noble prince within?'
  'He's up the stairs wi his bonny bride,
    An monny a lord and lady wi him.'

'O has he taen a bonny bride,   13
   An has he clean forgotten me!'
An sighing said that gay lady,
   I wish I were in my ain country!

But she's pitten her han in her pocket,   14
   An gin the porter guineas three;
Says, Take ye that, ye proud porter,
   An bid the bridegroom speak to me.

O whan the porter came up the stair,   15
   He's fa'n low down upon his knee:
'Won up, won up, ye proud porter,
   An what makes a' this courtesy?'

'O I've been porter at your gates   16
   This mair nor seven years an three,
But there is a lady at them now
   The like of whom I never did see.

'For on every finger she has a ring,   17
   An on the mid-finger she has three,
An there's as meikle goud aboon her brow
   As woud buy an earldome o lan to me.'

Then up it started Young Bicham,   18
   An sware so loud by Our Lady,
'It can be nane but Shusy Pye,
   That has come oer the sea to me.'

O quickly ran he down the stair,   19
   O fifteen steps he has made but three;
He's tane his bonny love in his arms,
   An a wot he kissd her tenderly.

'O hae you tane a bonny bride?   20
   An hae you quite forsaken me?
An hae ye quite forgotten her
   That gae you life an liberty?'

She's lookit oer her left shoulder   21
   To hide the tears stood in her ee;
'Now fare thee well, Young Bicham,' she says,
   'I'll strive to think nae mair on thee.'

22 Take back your daughter, madam,' he says,
       'An a double dowry I'll gi her wi;
    For I maun marry my first true love,
       That's done and suffered so much for me.'

23 He's take his bonny love by the han,
       And led her to yon fountain stane;
    He's changd her name frae Shusy Pye,
       An he's cald her his bonny love, Lady Jane.

[Ch 53C]   8. Young Bekie

(Young Beichan)

1   Young Bekie was as brave a knight
       As ever saild the sea;
    An he's doen him to the court of France,
       To serve for meat and fee.

2   He had nae been i the court of France
       A twelvemonth nor sae long,
    Til he fell in love with the king's daughter,
       An was thrown in prison strong.

3   The king he had but ae daughter,
       Burd Isbel was her name;
    An she has to the prison-house gane,
       To hear the prisoner's mane.

4   'O gin a lady woud borrow me,
       At her stirrup-foot I woud rin;
    Or gin a widow wad borrow me,
       I woud swear to be her son.

5   'Or gin a virgin woud borrow me,
       I woud wed her wi a ring;
    I'd gi her ha's, I'd gie her bowers,
       The bonny towrs o Linne.'

6   O barefoot, barefoot gaed she but,
       An barefoot came she ben;
    It was no for want o hose an shoone,
       Nor time to put them on.

But a' for fear that her father dear   7
   Had heard her making din:
She's stown the keys o the prison-house dor
   An latten the prisoner gang.

O whan she saw him, Young Bekie,   8
   Her heart was wondrous sair!
For the mice but an the bold rottons
   Had eaten his yallow hair.

She's gien him a shaver for his beard,   9
   A comber till his hair,
Five hunder pound in his pocket,
   To spen, an nae to spair.

She's gien him a steed was good in need,   10
   An a saddle o royal bone,
A leash o hounds o ae litter,
   An Hector called one.

Atween this twa a vow was made,   11
   'T was made full solemnly,
That or three years was come an gane,
   Well married they shoud be.

He had nae been in's ain country   12
   A twelvemonth till an end,
Till he's forcd to marry a duke's daughter,
   Or than lose a' his land.

'Ohon, alas!' says Young Beckie,   13
   'I know not what to dee;
For I canno win to Burd Isbel,
   And she kensnae to come to me.'

O it fell once upon a day   14
   Burd Isbel fell asleep,
An up it starts the Belly Blin,
   An stood at her bed-feet.

'O waken, waken, Burd Isbel,   15
   How [can] you sleep so soun,
When this is Bekie's wedding day,
   An the marriage gain on?

16   'Ye do ye to your mither's bowr,
           Think neither sin nor shame;
       An ye tak twa o your mither's marys,
           To keep ye frae thinking lang.

17   'Ye dress yoursel in the red scarlet,
           An your marys in dainty green,
       An ye pit girdles about your middles
           Would buy an earldome.

18   'O ye gang down by yon sea-side,
           An down by yon sea-stran;
       Sae bonny will the Hollans boats
           Come rowin till your han.

19   'Ye set your milk-white foot abord,
           Cry, Hail ye, Domine!
       An I shal be the steerer o't,
           To row you oer the sea.'

20   She's tane her till her mither's bowr,
           Thought neither sin nor shame,
       An she took twa o her mither's marys,
           To keep her frae thinking lang.

21   She dressd hersel i the red scarlet,
           Her marys i dainty green,
       And they pat girdles about their middles
           Would buy an earldome.

22   An they gid down by yon sea-side,
           An down by yon sea-stran;
       Sae bonny did the Hollan boats
           Come rowin to their han.

23   She set her milk-white foot on board,
           Cried, Hail ye, Domine!
       An the Belly Blin was the steerer o't,
           To row her oer the sea.

24   Whan she came to Young Bekie's gate,
           She heard the music play;
       Sae well she kent frae a' she heard,
           It was his wedding day.

She's pitten her han in her pocket,   25
   Gin the porter guineas three;
'Hae, tak ye that, ye proud porter,
   Bid the bride-groom speake to me.'

O whan that he cam up the stair,   26
   He fell low down on his knee:
He haild the king, an he haild the queen,
   An he haild him, Young Bekie.

'O I've been porter at your gates   27
   This thirty years an three;
But there's three ladies at them now,
   Their like I never did see.

'There's ane o them dressd in red scarlet,   28
   And twa in dainty green,
An they hae girdles about their middles
   Woud buy an earldome.'

Then out it spake the bierly bride,   29
   Was a' goud to the chin;
'Gin she be braw without,' she says,
   'We's be as braw within.'

Then up it starts him, Young Bekie,   30
   An the tears was in his ee:
'I'll lay my life it's Burd Isbel,
   Come oer the sea to me.'

O quickly ran he down the stair,   31
   An whan he saw 't was shee,
He kindly took her in his arms,
   And kissd her tenderly.

'O hae ye forgotten, Young Bekie,   32
   The vow ye made to me,
Whan I took you out o the prison strong,
   Whan ye was condemnd to die?

'I gae you a steed was good in need,   33
   An a saddle o royal bone,
A leash o hounds o ae litter,
   An Hector called one.'

34   It was well kent what the lady said,
            That it wasnae a lee,
        For at ilka word the lady spake,
            The hound fell at her knee.

35   'Tak hame, tak hame your daughter dear,
            A blessing gae her wi,
        For I maun marry my Burd Isbel,
            That's come oer the sea to me.'

36   'Is this the custom o your house,
            Or the fashion o your lan,
        To marry a maid in a May mornin,
            An send her back at even?'

[*Ch 62E*]   9. Fair Annie

1   'O wha will bake my bridal bread,
            And brew my bridal ale?
        Wha will welcome my bright bride,
            That I bring oer the dale?'

2   'O I will bake your bridal bread,
            An brew your bridal ale;
        An I will welcome your bright bride,
            That you bring oer the dale.

3   'O she that welcomes my bright bride
            Maun gang like maiden fair;
        She maun lace her in her green cloathin,
            An braid her yallow hair.'

4   'O how can I gang maiden like,
            Whan maiden I am nane?
        Whan I ha born you seven sons,
            An am wi bairn again?'

5   The lady stood in her bowr door
            An lookit oer the lan,
        An there she saw her ain good lord,
            Leadin his bride by the han.

She's dressd her sons i the scarlet red,   6
    Hersel i the dainty green,
An tho her cheek lookd pale and wan,
    She well might ha been a queen.

She calld upon her eldest son: 7
    'Look yonder what you see;
For yonder comes your father dear,
    Your step-mother him wi.

'O you'r welcome hame, my ain good lord,   8
    To your ha's but an your bowrs;
You'r welcome hame, my ain good lord,
    To your castles an your towrs:
Sae is your bright bride you beside,
    She's fairer nor the flowers.'

'O whatn a lady's that?' she says,   9
    'That welcoms you an me?
If I'm lang lady about this place,
    Some good I will her dee.
She looks sae like my sister Jane,
    Was stoln i the bowr frae me.'

O she has servd the lang tables,   10
    Wi the white bread an the wine;
But ay she drank the wan water,
    To keep her colour fine.

An she gid by the first table,   11
    An leugh amo them a';
But ere she reachd the second table,
    She let the tears down fa.

She's taen a napkin lang an white,   12
    An hung't upon a pin;
It was to dry her watry eyes,
    As she went out and in.

Whan bells were rung, an mass was sung,   13
    An a' man boun to bed,
The bride but an the bonny bridegroom
    In ae chamber was laid.

14   She's taen her harp intill her han,
         To harp this twa asleep;
      An ay as she harped an she sang,
         Full sorely did she weep.

15   'O seven fu fair sons I have born
         To the good lord o this place,
      An I wish that they were seven hares,
         To run the castle race,
      An I mysel a good gray houn,
         An I woud gi them chase.

16   'O seven fu fair sons I have born
         To the good lord o this ha;
      I wish that they were seven rottons,
         To rin the castle wa,
      An I mysell a good gray cat,
         I wot I woud worry them a'.

17   'The earle o Richmond was my father,
         An the lady was my mother,
      An a' the bairns bisides mysel
         Was a sister an a brother.'

18   'Sing on, sing on, ye gay lady,
         I wot ye hae sung in time;
      Gin the earle o Richmond was your father,
         I wot sae was he mine.'

19   'Rise up, rise up, my bierly bride;
         I think my bed's but caul;
      I woudna hear my lady lament
         For your tocher ten times taul.

20   'O seven ships did bring you here,
         An an sal tak you hame;
      The leve I'll keep to your sister Jane,
         For tocher she gat nane.'

10. Child Waters [Ch 63B]

'I warn ye all, ye gay ladies,   1
   That wear scarlet an brown,
That ye dinna leave your father's house,
   To follow young men frae town.'

'O here am I, a lady gay,   2
   That wears scarlet an brown,
Yet I will leave my father's house,
   An follow Lord John frae the town.'

Lord John stood in his stable-door,   3
   Said he was bound to ride;
Burd Ellen stood in her bowr-door,
   Said she'd rin by his side.

He's pitten on his cork-heeld shoone,   4
   An fast awa rade he;
She's clade hersel in page array,
   An after him ran she.

Till they came till a wan water,   5
   An folks do ca it Clyde;
Then he's lookit oer his left shoulder,
   Says, Lady, can ye wide?

'O I learnt it i my father house,   6
An I learnt it for my weal,
Wenneer I came to a wan water,
   To swim like ony eel.'

But the firstin stap the lady stappit,   7
   The water came til her knee;
'Ohon, alas!' said the lady,
   'This water's oer deep for me.'

The nextin stap the lady stappit,   8
   The water came till her middle;
An sighin says that gay lady,
   I've wat my gouden girdle.

The nextin stap the lady stappit,   9
   The water came till her pap;
An the bairn that was in her twa sides
   For caul began to quake.

10   'Lye still, lye still, my ain dear babe,
          Ye work your mither wae;
       Your father rides on high horse-back,
          Cares little for us twae.'

11   O about the midst o Clyden water
          There was a yeard-fast stane;
       He lightly turnd his horse about,
          An took her on him behin.

12   'O tell me this now, good Lord John,
          An a word ye dinna lee,
       How far it is to your lodgin,
          Whare we this night maun be?'

13   'O see you nae yon castle, Ellen,
          That shines sae fair to see?
       There is a lady in it, Ellen,
          Will sunder you an me.

14   'There is a lady in that castle
          Will sunder you and I:'
       'Betide me well, betide me wae,
          I sal go there an try.'

15   'O my dogs sal eat the good white bread,
          An ye sal eat the bran;
       Then will ye sigh, an say, alas!
          That ever I was a man!'

16   'O I sal eat the good white bread,
          An your dogs sal eat the bran;
       An I hope to live an bless the day,
          That ever ye was a man.'

17   'O my horse sal eat the good white meal,
          An ye sal eat the corn;
       Then will ye curse the heavy hour
          That ever your love was born.'

18   'O I sal eat the good white meal,
          An your horse sal eat the corn;
       An I ay sall bless the happy hour
          That ever my love was born.'

O four an twenty gay ladies   19
   Welcomd Lord John to the ha,
But a fairer lady then them a'
   Led his horse to the stable sta.

An four an twenty gay ladies   20
   Welcomd Lord John to the green,
But a fairer lady than them a'
   At the manger stood alane.

Whan bells were rung, an mass was sung,   21
   An a' men boun to meat,
Burd Ellen at a bye-table
   Amo the foot-men was set.

'O eat an drink, my bonny boy,   22
   The white bread an the beer:'
'The never a bit can I eat or drink,
   My heart's sae full of fear.'

'O eat an drink, my bonny boy,   23
   The white bread an the wine:'
'O I canna eat nor drink, master,
   My heart's sae full of pine.'

But out it spake Lord John's mother,   24
   An a wise woman was she:
'Whare met ye wi that bonny boy,
   That looks sae sad on thee?

'Sometimes his cheek is rosy red,   25
   An sometimes deadly wan;
He's liker a woman big wi bairn,
   Than a young lord's serving man.'

'O it makes me laugh, my mother dear, 26
   Sic words to hear fra thee;
He is a squire's ae dearest son,
   That for love has followd me.

'Rise up, rise up, my bonny boy,   27
   Gi my horse corn an hay:'
'O that I will, my master dear,
   As quickly as I may.'

28   She's taen the hay under her arm,
          The corn intill her han,
      An she's gane to the great stable,
          As fast as eer she can.

29   'O room ye roun, my bonny broun steeds,
          O room ye near the wa;
      For the pain that strikes me thro my sides
          Full soon will gar me fa.'

30   She's leand her back against the wa;
          Strong travail seizd her on;
      An even amo the great horse feet
          Burd Ellen brought forth her son.

31   Lord John'[s] mither intill her bowr
          Was sitting all alone,
      Whan, i the silence o the night,
          She heard fair Ellen's moan.

32   'Won up, won up, my son,' she says,
          'Go se how a' does fare;
      For I think I hear a woman's groans,
          An a bairn greeting sair.'

33   O hastily he gat him up,
          Stayd neither for hose nor shoone,
      An he's doen him to the stable-door,
          Wi the clear light o the moon.

34   He strack the door hard wi his foot,
          An sae has he wi his knee,
      An iron locks an iron bars
          Into the floor flung he:
      'Be not afraid, Burd Ellen, 'he says,
          'Ther's nane come in but me.'

35   Up he has taen his bonny young son,
          An gard wash him wi the milk;
      An up has he taen his fair lady,
          Gard row her in the silk.

39

'Cheer up your heart, Burd Ellen,' he says,   36
    'Look nae mair sad nor wae;
For your marriage an your kirkin too
    Sal baith be in ae day.'

11. Lady Maisry   [*Ch 65A*]

The young lords o the north country   1
    Have all a wooing gone,
To win the love of Lady Maisry,
    But o them she woud hae none.

O they hae courted Lady Maisry   2
    Wi a' kin kind of things;
An they hae sought her Lady Maisry
    Wi brotches an wi' rings.

An they ha sought her Lady Maisry   3
    Frae father and frae mother;
An they ha sought her Lady Maisry
    Frae sister an frae brother.

An they ha followd her Lady Maisry   4
    Thro chamber an thro ha;
But a' that they coud say to her,
    Her answer still was Na.

'O had your tongues, young men,' she says,   5
    'An think nae mair o me;
For I've gien my love to an English lord,
    An think nae mair o me.'

Her father's kitchy-boy heard that,   6
    An ill death may he dee!
An he is on to her brother,
    As fast as gang coud he.

'O is my father an my mother well,   7
    But an my brothers three?
Gin my sister Lady Maisry be well,
    There's naething can ail me.'

8   'Your father and your mother is well,
            But an your brothers three;
        Your sister Lady Maisry's well,
            So big wi bairn gangs she.'

9   'Gin this be true you tell to me,
            My mailison light on thee!
        But gin it be a lie you tell,
            You sal be hangit hie.'

10   He's done him to his sister's bowr,
            Wi meikle doole an care;
        An there he saw her Lady Maisry,
            Kembing her yallow hair.

11   'O wha is aught that bairn,' he says,
            'That ye sae big are wi?
        And gin ye winna own the truth,
            This moment ye sall dee.'

12   She turned her right an roun about,
            An the kem fell frae her han;
        A trembling seizd her fair body,
            An her rosy cheek grew wan.

13   'O pardon me, my brother dear,
            An the truth I'll tell to thee;
        My bairn it is to Lord William,
            An he is betrothd to me.'

14   'O coud na ye gotten dukes, or lords,
            Intill your ain country,
        That ye draw up wi an English dog,
            To bring this shame on me?

15   'But ye maun gi up the English lord,
            Whan youre young babe is born;
        For, gin you keep by him an hour langer,
            Your life sall be forlorn.'

16   'I will gi up this English blood,
            Till my young babe be born;
        But the never a day nor hour langer,
            Tho my life should be forlorn.'

41

'O whare is a' my merry young men,   17
  Whom I gi meat and fee,
To pu the thistle and the thorn,
  To burn this wile whore wi?'

'O whare will I get a bonny boy,   18
  To help me in my need,
To rin wi hast to Lord William,
  And bid him come wi speed?'

O out it spake a bonny boy,   19
  Stood by her brother's side:
'O I would rin your errand, lady,
  Oer a' the world wide.

'Aft have I run your errands, lady,   20
  Whan blawn baith win and weet;
But now I'll rin your errand, lady,
  Wi sat tears on my cheek.'

O whan he came to broken briggs,   21
  He bent his bow and swam,
An whan he came to the green grass growin,
  He slackd his shoone and ran.

O whan he came to Lord William's gates,   22
  He baed na to chap or ca,
But set his bent bow till his breast,
  An lightly lap the wa;
An, or the porter was at the gate,
  The boy was i the ha.

'O is my biggins broken, boy?   23
  Or is my towers won?
Or is my lady lighter yet,
  Of a dear daughter or son?'

'Your biggin is na broken, sir,   24
  Nor is your towers won;
But the fairest lady in a' the lan
  For you this day maun burn.'

25   'O saddle me the black, the black,
         Or saddle me the brown;
     O saddle me the swiftest steed
         That ever rade frae a town.'

26   Or he was near a mile awa,
         She heard his wild horse sneeze:
     'Mend up the fire, my false brother,
         It's na come to my knees.'

27   O whan he lighted at the gate,
         She heard his bridle ring:
     'Mend up the fire, my false brother,
         It's far yet frae my chin.

28   'Mend up the fire to me, brother,
         Mend up the fire to me;
     For I see him comin hard an fast
         Will soon men't up to thee.

29   'O gin my hands had been loose, Willy,
         Sae hard as they are boun,
     I would have turnd me frae the gleed,
         And castin out your young son.'

30   'O I'll gar burn for you, Maisry,
         Your father an your mother;
     An I'll gar burn for you, Maisry,
         Your sister an your brother.

31   'An I'll gar burn for you, Maisry,
         The chief of a' your kin;
     An the last bonfire that I come to,
         Mysel I will cast in.'

12. The Lass of Roch Royal   [Ch 76D]

'O wha will shoe my fu fair foot?   1
   An wha will glove my han?
An wha will lace my middle gimp
   Wi the new made London ban?

'Or wha will kemb my yallow hair,   2
   Wi the new made silver kemb?
Or wha'll be father to my young bairn,
   Till Love Gregor come hame?'

Her father shoed her fu fair foot,   3
   Her mother glovd her han;
Her sister lac'd her middle gimp
   Wi the new made London ban.

Her brother kembd her yallow hair,   4
   Wi the new made silver kemb,
But the king o heaven maun father her bairn,
   Till Love Gregor come hame.

'O gin I had a bony ship,   5
   An men to sail wi me,
It's I would gang to my true-love,
   Since he winna come to me.'

Her father's gien her a bonny ship,   6
   An sent her to the stran;
She's tane her young son in her arms,
   An turnd her back to the lan.

She had na been on the sea saillin   7
   About a month or more,
Till landed has she her bonny ship
   Near her true-love's door.

The night was dark, an the win blew caul,   8
   An her love was fast asleep,
An the bairn that was in her twa arms
   Fu sair began to weep.

9   Long stood she at her true-love's door,
         An lang tirld at the pin;
     At length up gat his fa'se mither,
         Says, Wha's that woud be in?

10   'O it is Anny of Roch-royal,
         Your love, come oer the sea,
     But an your young son in her arms;
         So open the door to me.'

11   'Awa, awa, you ill woman,
         You've na come here for gude,
     You're but a witch, or wile warlock,
         Or mermaid o the flude.'

12   'I'm na a witch, or wile warlock,
         Nor mermaiden,' said she;
     'I'm but Fair Anny o Roch-royal;
         O open the door to me.'

13   'O gin ye be Anny o Roch-royal,
         As [I] trust not ye be,
     What taiken can ye gie that ever
         I kept your company?'

14   'O dinna ye mind, Love Gregor,' she says,
         'Whan we sat at the wine,
     How we changed the napkins frae our necks,
         It's na sae lang sin syne?

15   'An yours was good, an good enough,
         But nae sae good as mine;
     For yours was o the cumbruk clear,
         But mine was silk sae fine.

16   'An dinna ye mind, Love Gregor,' she says,
         'As we twa sat at dine,
     How we changed the rings frae our fingers,
         But ay the best was mine?

17   'For yours was good, an good enough,
         Yet nae sae good as mine;
     For yours was of the good red gold,
         But mine o the diamonds fine.

45

'Sae open the door now, Love Gregor, 18
  An open it wi speed,
Or your young son that is in my arms
  For cauld will soon be dead.'

'Awa, awa, you ill woman, 19
  Gae frae my door for shame;
For I hae gotten another fair love,
  Sae ye may hye you hame.'

'O hae you gotten another fair love, 20
  For a' the oaths you sware?
Then fair you well now, fa'se Gregor,
  For me you's never see mair.'

O heely, heely gi'd she back, 21
  As the day began to peep;
She set her foot on good ship-board,
  An sair, sair did she weep.

Love Gregor started frae his sleep, 22
  An to his mither did say,
I dreamd a dream this night, mither,
  That maks my heart right wae.

'I dreamd that Anny of Roch-royal, 23
  The flowr o a' her kin,
Was standin mournin at my door,
  But nane would lat her in.'

'O there was a woman stood at the door, 24
  Wi a bairn intill her arms,
But I woud na lat her within the bowr,
  For fear she had done you harm.'

O quickly, quickly raise he up, 25
  An fast ran to the stran,
An there he saw her Fair Anny,
  Was sailin frae the lan.

An 'Heigh, Anny!' an 'Hou, Anny! 26
  O Anny, speak to me!'
But ay the louder that he cried Anny,
  The louder roard the sea.

27   An 'Heigh, Anny!' an 'Hou, Anny!
      O Anny, winna you bide?'
      But ay the langer that he cried Anny,
      The higher roard the tide.

28   The win grew loud, an the sea grew rough,
      An the ship was rent in twain,
      An soon he saw her Fair Anny
      Come floating oer the main.

29   He saw his young son in her arms,
      Baith tossd aboon the tide;
      He wrang his hands, than fast he ran,
      An plung'd i the sea sae wide.

30   He catchd her by the yellow hair,
      An drew her to the strand,
      But cauld an stiff was every limb
      Before he reachd the land.

31   O first he kissd her cherry cheek,
      An then he kissd her chin;
      An sair he kissd her ruby lips,
      But there was nae breath within.

32   O he has mournd oer Fair Anny
      Till the sun was gaing down,
      Then wi a sigh his heart it brast,
      An his soul to heaven has flown.

[Ch 76E]   13. Love Gregor
             (The Lass of Roch Royal)

1   'O wha will shoe my fu fair foot?
      And wha will glove my hand?
      And wha will lace my middle jimp,
      Wi the new made London band?

2   'And wha will kaim my yellow hair,
      Wi the new made silver kaim?
      And wha will father my young son,
      Till Love Gregor come hame?'

'Your father will shoe your fu fair foot,   3
    Your mother will glove your hand;
Your sister will lace your middle jimp
    Wi the new made London band.

'Your brother will kaim your yellow hair,   4
    Wi the new made silver kaim;
And the king of heaven will father your bairn,
    Till Love Gregor come haim.'

'But I will get a bonny boat,   5
    And I will sail the sea,
For I maun gang to Love Gregor,
    Since he canno come hame to me.'

O she has gotten a bonny boat,   6
    And sailld the sa't sea fame;
She langd to see her ain true-love,
    Since he could no come hame.

'O row your boat, my mariners,   7
    And bring me to the land,
For yonder I see my love's castle,
    Closs by the sa't sea strand.'

She has taen her young son in her arms,   8
    And to the door she's gone,
And lang she's knocked and sair she ca'd,
    But answer got she none.

'O open the door, Love Gregor,' she says,   9
    'O open, and let me in;
For the wind blaws thro my yellow hair,
    And the rain draps oer my chin.'

'Awa, awa, ye ill woman,   10
    You'r nae come here for good;
You'r but some witch, or wile warlock,
    Or mer-maid of the flood.'

'I am neither a witch nor a wile warlock,   11
    Nor mer-maid of the sea,
I am Fair Annie of Rough Royal;
    O open the door to me.'

12   'Gin ye be Annie of Rough Royal –
            And I trust ye are not she –
        Now tell me some of the love-tokens
            That past between you and me.'

13   'O dinna you mind now, Love Gregor,
            When we sat at the wine,
        How we changed the rings frae our fingers?
            And I can show thee thine.

14   'O yours was good, and good enneugh,
            But ay the best was mine;
        For yours was o the good red goud,
            But mine of the dimonds fine.

15   'But open the door now, Love Gregor,
            O open the door I pray,
        For your young son that is in my arms
            Will be dead ere it be day.'

16   'Awa, awa, ye ill woman,
            For here ye shanno win in;
        Gae drown ye in the raging sea,
            Or hang on the gallows-pin.'

17   When the cock had crawn, and day did dawn,
            And the sun began to peep,
        Then it raise him Love Gregor,
            And sair, sair did he weep.

18   'O I dreamd a dream, my mother dear,
            The thoughts o it gars me greet,
        That Fair Annie of Rough Royal
            Lay cauld dead at my feet.'

19   'Gin it be for Annie of Rough Royal
            That ye make a' this din,
        She stood a' last night at this door,
            But I trow she wan no in.'

20   'O wae betide ye, ill woman,
            An ill dead may ye die!
        That ye woudno open the door to her,
            Nor yet woud waken me.'

O he has gone down to yon shore-side,   21
    As fast as he could fare;
He saw Fair Annie in her boat,
    But the wind it tossd her sair.

And 'Hey, Annie!' and 'How, Annie!   22
    O Annie, winna ye bide?'
But ay the mair that he cried Annie,
    The braider grew the tide.

And 'Hey, Annie!' and 'How, Annie!   23
    Dear Annie, speak to me!'
But ay the louder he cried Annie,
    The louder roard the sea.

The wind blew loud, the sea grew rough,   24
    And dashd the boat on shore;
Fair Annie floats on the raging sea.
    But her young son raise no more.

Love Gregor tare his yellow hair,   25
    And made a heavy moan;
Fair Annie's corpse lay at his feet,
    But his bonny young son was gone.

O cherry, cherry was her cheek,   26
    And gowden was her hair,
But clay cold were her rosey lips,
    Nae spark of life was there.

And first he's kissd her cherry cheek,   27
    And neist he's kissed her chin;
And saftly pressd her rosey lips,
    But there was nae breath within.

'O wae betide my cruel mother,   28
    And an ill dead may she die!
For she turnd my true-love frae my door,
    When she came sae far to me.'

14. Fause Foodrage

1   King Easter has courted her for her gowd,
        King Wester for her fee,
    King Honor for her lands sae braid,
        And for her fair body.

2   They had not been four months married,
        As I have heard them tell,
    Until the nobles of the land
        Against them did rebel.

3   And they cast kaivles them amang,
        And kaivles them between,
    And they cast kaivles them amang
        Wha shoud gae kill the king.

4   O some said yea, and some said nay,
        Their words did not agree;
    Till up it gat him Fa'se Footrage,
        And sware it shoud be he.

5   When bells were rung, and mass was sung,
        And a' man boon to bed,
    King Honor and his gay ladie
        In a hie chamer were laid.

6   Then up it raise him Fa'se Footrage,
        While a' were fast asleep,
    And slew the porter in his lodge,
        That watch and ward did keep.

7   O four and twenty silver keys
        Hang hie upon a pin,
    And ay as a door he did unlock,
        He has fastend it him behind.

8   Then up it raise him King Honor,
        Says, What means a' this din!
    Now what's the matter, Fa'se Footrage?
        O wha was't loot you in?

9   'O ye my errand well shall learn
        Before that I depart;'
    Then drew a knife baith lang and sharp
        And pierced him thro the heart.

Then up it got the Queen hersell,   10
   And fell low down on her knee:
'O spare my life now, Fa'se Footrage!
   For I never injured thee.

'O spare my life now, Fa'se Footrage!   11
   Until I lighter be,
And see gin it be lad or lass
   King Honor has left me wi.'

'O gin it be a lass,' he says,   12
   'Well nursed she shall be;
But gin it be a lad-bairn,
   He shall be hanged hie.

'I winna spare his tender age,   13
   Nor yet his hie, hie kin;
But as soon as eer he born is,
   He shall mount the gallows-pin.'

O four and twenty valiant knights   14
   Were set the Queen to guard,
And four stood ay at her bower-door,
   To keep baith watch and ward.

But when the time drew till an end   15
   That she should lighter be,
She cast about to find a wile
   To set her body free.

O she has birled these merry young men   16
   Wi strong beer and wi wine,
Until she made them a' as drunk
   As any wallwood swine.

'O narrow, narrow is this window,   17
   And big, big am I grown!'
Yet thro the might of Our Ladie
   Out at it she has won.

She wanderd up, she wanderd down,   18
   She wanderd out and in,
And at last, into the very swines' stye,
   The Queen brought forth a son.

19   Then they cast kaivles them amang
     Wha should gae seek the Queen,
   And the kaivle fell upon Wise William,
     And he's sent his wife for him.

20   O when she saw Wise William's wife,
     The Queen fell on her knee;
   'Win up, win up, madame,' she says,
     'What means this courtesie?'

21   'O out of this I winna rise
     Till a boon ye grant to me,
   To change your lass for this lad-bairn
     King Honor left me wi.

22   'And ye maun learn my gay gose-hawke
     Well how to breast a steed,
   And I shall learn your turtle-dow
     As well to write and read.

23   'And ye maun learn my gay gose-hawke
     To wield baith bow and brand,
   And I shall learn your turtle-dow
     To lay gowd wi her hand.

24   'At kirk or market where we meet,
     We dare nae mair avow
   But, Dame how does my gay gose-hawk?
     Madame, how does my dow?'

25   When days were gane, and years came on,
     Wise William he thought long;
   Out has he taen King Honor's son,
     A hunting for to gang.

26   It sae fell out at their hunting,
     Upon a summer's day,
   That they cam by a fair castle,
     Stood on a sunny brae.

27   'O dinna ye see that bonny castle,
     Wi wa's and towers sae fair?
   Gin ilka man had back his ain,
     Of it you shoud be heir.'

'How I shoud be heir of that castle   28
  In sooth I canna see,
When it belongs to Fa'se Footrage,
  And he's nae kin to me.'

'O gin ye shoud kill him Fa'se Footrage,   29
  You woud do what is right;
For I wot he killd your father dear,
  Ere ever you saw the light.

'Gin ye should kill him Fa'se Footrage,   30
  There is nae man durst you blame;
For he keeps your mother a prisoner,
  And she dares no take you hame.'

The boy stared wild like a gray gose-hawke, 31
  Says, What may a' this mean!
'My boy, you are King Honor's son,
  And your mother's our lawful queen.'

'O gin I be King Honor's son,   32
  By Our Ladie I swear,
This day I will that traytour slay,
  And relieve my mother dear.'

He has set his bent bow till his breast,   33
  And lap the castle-wa,
And soon he's siesed on Fa'se Footrage,
  Wha loud for help gan ca.

'O hold your tongue now, Fa'se Footrage,   34
  Frae me you shanno flee;'
Syne pierced him through the foul fa'se heart,
  And set his mother free.

And he has rewarded Wise William   35
  Wi the best half of his land,
And sae has he the turtle-dow
  Wi the truth of his right hand.

15. Fair Mary of
                    Wallington

1   'O we were sisters seven, Maisry,
             And five are dead wi child;
         There is nane but you and I, Maisry,
             And we'll go maidens mild.'

2   She hardly had the word spoken,
             And turnd her round about,
         When the bonny Earl of Livingston
             Was calling Maisry out.

3   Upon a bonny milk-white steed,
             That drank out of the Tyne,
         And a' was for her Ladie Maisry,
             To take her hyne and hyne.

4   Upon a bonny milk-white steed,
             That drank out o the Tay,
         And a' was for her Lady Maisry,
             To carry her away.

5   She had not been at Livingston
             A twelve month and a day,
         Until she was as big wi bairn
             As any ladie coud gae.

6   She calld upon her little foot-page,
             Says, Ye maun run wi speed,
         And bid my mother come to me,
             For of her I'll soon have need.

7   'See, there is the brootch frae my hause-bane,
             It is of gowd sae ried;
         Gin she winna come when I'm alive,
             Bid her come when I am dead.'

8   But ere she wan to Livingston,
             As fast as she coud ride,
         The gaggs they were in Maisry's mouth,
             And the sharp sheers in her side.

Her good lord wrang his milk-white hands, 9
  Till the gowd rings flaw in three:
'Let ha's and bowers and a' gae waste,
  My bonny love's taen frae me!'

'O hold your tongue, Lord Livingston, 10
  Let a' your mourning be;
For I bare the bird between my sides,
  Yet I maun thole her to die.'

Then out it spake her sister dear, 11
  As she sat at her head:
'That man is not in Christendoom
  Shall gar me die sicken dead.'

'O hold your tongue, my ae daughter, 12
  Let a' your folly be,
For ye shall be married ere this day week
  Tho the same death you should die.'

16. Lamkin [*Ch 93A*]

It's Lamkin was a mason good 1
  as ever built wi stane;
He built Lord Wearie's castle,
  but payment got he nane.

'O pay me, Lord Wearie, 2
  come, pay me my fee:'
'I canna pay you, Lamkin,
  for I maun gang oer the sea.'

'O pay me now, Lord Wearie, 3
  come, pay me out o hand:'
'I canna pay you, Lamkin,
  unless I sell my land.'

'O gin ye winna pay me, 4
  I here sall mak a vow,
Before that ye come hame again,
  ye sall hae cause to rue.'

5   Lord Wearie got a bonny ship,
           to sail the saut sea faem;
      Bade his lady weel the castle keep,
           ay till he should come hame.

6   But the nourice was a fause limmer
           as eer hung on a tree;
      She laid a plot wi Lamkin,
           whan her lord was oer the sea.

7   She laid a plot wi Lamkin,
           when the servants were awa,
      Loot him in at a little shot-window,
           and brought him to the ha.

8   'O whare's a' the men o this house,
           that ca me Lamkin?'
      'They're at the barn-well thrashing;
           't will be lang ere they come in.'

9   'And whare's the women o this house,
           that ca me Lamkin?'
      'They're at the far well washing;
           't will be lang ere they come in.'

10   'And whare's the bairns o this house,
           that ca me Lamkin?'
      'They're at the school reading;
           't will be night or they come hame.'

11   'O whare's the lady o this house,
           that ca's me Lamkin?'
      'She's up in her bower sewing,
           but we soon can bring her down.'

12   Then Lamkin's tane a sharp knife,
           that hang down by his gaire,
      And he has gien the bonny babe
           a deep wound and a sair.

13   Then Lamkin he rocked,
           and the fause nourice sang,
      Till frae ilkae bore o the cradle
           the red blood out sprang.

Then out it spak the lady,   14
    as she stood on the stair:
'What ails my bairn, nourice,
    that he's greeting sae sair?

'O still my bairn, nourice,   15
    O still him wi the pap!'
'He winna still, lady,
    for this nor for that.'

'O still my bairn, nourice,   16
    O still him wi the wand!'
'He winna still, lady,
    for a' his father's land.'

'O still my bairn, nourice,   17
    O still him wi the bell!'
'He winna still, lady,
    till ye come down yoursel.'

O the firsten step she steppit,   18
    she steppit on a stane;
But the neisten step she steppit,
    she met him Lamkin.

'O mercy, mercy, Lamkin,   19
    hae mercy upon me!
Though you've taen my young son's life,
    ye may let mysel be.'

'O sall I kill her, nourice,   20
    or sall I lat her be?'
'O kill her, kill her, Lamkin,
    for she neer was good to me.'

'O scour the bason, nourice,   21
    and mak it fair and clean,
For to keep this lady's heart's blood,
    for she's come o noble kin.'

'There need nae bason, Lamkin,   22
    lat it run through the floor;
What better is the heart's blood
    o the rich than o the poor?'

23   But ere three months were at an end,
         Lord Wearie came again;
     But dowie, dowie was his heart
         when first he came hame.

24   'O wha's blood is this,' he says,
         'that lies in the chamer?'
     'It is your lady's heart's blood;
         'tis as clear as the lamer.'

25   'And wha's blood is this,' he says,
         'that lies in my ha?'
     'It is your young son's heart's blood;
         't is the clearest ava.'

26   O sweetly sang the black-bird
         that sat upon the tree;
     But sairer grat Lamkin,
         when he was condemnd to die.

27   And bonny sang the mavis,
         out o the thorny brake;
     But sairer grat the nourice,
         when she was tied to the stake.

[*Ch 96A*]   17. The Gay Goshawk

1   'O well's me o my gay goss-hawk,
         That he can speak and flee;
     He'll carry a letter to my love,
         Bring back another to me.'

2   'O how can I your true-love ken,
         Or how can I her know?
     Whan frae her mouth I never heard couth,
         Nor wi my eyes her saw.'

3   'O well sal ye my true-love ken,
         As soon as you her see;
     For, of a' the flowrs in fair Englan,
         The fairest flowr is she.

'At even at my love's bowr-door   4
    There grows a bowing birk,
An sit ye down and sing thereon,
    As she gangs to the kirk.

'An four-and-twenty ladies fair   5
    Will wash and go to kirk,
But well shall ye my true-love ken,
    For she wears goud on her skirt.

'An four and twenty gay ladies   6
    Will to the mass repair,
But well sal ye my true-love ken,
    For she wears goud on her hair.'

O even at that lady's bowr-door   7
    There grows a bowin birk,
An she set down and sang thereon,
    As she ged to the kirk.

'O eet and drink, my marys a',   8
    The wine flows you among,
Till I gang to my shot-window,
    An hear yon bonny bird's song.

'Sing on, sing on, my bonny bird,   9
    The song ye sang the streen,
For I ken by your sweet singin
    You're frae my true-love sen.'

O first he sang a merry song,   10
    An then he sang a grave,
An then he peckd his feathers gray,
    To her the letter gave.

'Ha, there's a letter frae your love,   11
    He says he sent you three;
He canna wait your love langer,
    But for your sake he'll die.

'He bids you write a letter to him;   12
    He says he's sent you five;
He canno wait your love langer,
    Tho you're the fairest woman alive.'

13   'Ye bid him bake his bridal-bread,
         And brew his bridal-ale,
      An I'll meet him in fair Scotlan
         Lang, lang or it be stale.'

14   She's doen her to her father dear,
         Fa'n low down on her knee:
      'A boon, a boon, my father dear,
         I pray you, grant it me.'

15   'Ask on, ask on, my daughter,
         An granted it sal be;
      Except ae squire in fair Scotlan,
         An him you sall never see.'

16   'The only boon, my father dear,
         That I do crave of the,
      Is, gin I die in southin lands,
         In Scotland to bury me.

17   'An the firstin kirk that ye come till,
         Ye gar the bells be rung,
      An the nextin kirk that ye come till,
         Ye gar the mess be sung.

18   'An the thirdin kirk that ye come till,
         You deal gold for my sake,
      An the fourthin kirk that ye come till,
         You tarry there till night.'

19   She is doen her to her bigly bowr,
         As fast as she coud fare,
      An she has tane a sleepy draught,
         That she had mixed wi care.

20   She's laid her down upon her bed,
         An soon she's fa'n asleep,
      And soon oer every tender limb
         Cauld death began to creep.

21   Whan night was flown, an day was come,
         Nae ane that did her see
      But thought she was as surely dead
         As ony lady coud be.

Her father an her brothers dear   22
   Gard make to her a bier;
The tae half was o guide red gold,
   The tither o silver clear.

Her mither an her sisters fair   23
   Gard work for her a sark;
The tae half was o cambrick fine,
   The tither o needle wark.

The firstin kirk that they came till,   24
   They gard the bells be rung,
An the nextin kirk that they came till,
   They gard the mess be sung.

The thirdin kirk that they came till,   25
   They dealt gold for her sake,
An the fourthin kirk that they came till,
   Lo, there they met her make!

'Lay down, lay down the bigly bier,   26
   Lat me the dead look on;'
Wi cherry cheeks and ruby lips
   She lay an smil'd on him.

'O ae sheave o your bread, true-love,   27
   An ae glass o your wine,
For I hae fasted for your sake
   These fully days is nine.

'Gang hame, gang hame, my seven bold brothers,   28
   Gang hame and sound your horn;
An ye may boast in southin lans
   Your sister's playd you scorn.'

18. Brown Robin   [*Ch 97A*]

The king but an his nobles a' ⎫ *bis*   1
   Sat birling at the wine; ⎭
He would ha nane but his ae daughter
   To wait on them at dine.

2 She's served them butt, she's servd them ben,
  Intill a gown of green,
 But her ee was ay on Brown Robin,
  That stood low under the rain.

3 She's doen her to her bigly bowr,
  As fast as she coud gang,
 An there she's drawn her shot-window,
  An she's harped an she sang.

4 'There sits a bird i my father's garden,
  An O but she sings sweet!
 I hope to live an see the day
  Whan wi my love I'll meet.'

5 'O gin that ye like me as well
  As your tongue tells to me,
 What hour o the night, my lady bright,
  At your bowr sal I be?'

6 'Whan my father an gay Gilbert
  Are baith set at the wine,
 O ready, ready I will be
  To lat my true-love in.'

7 O she has birld her father's porter
  Wi strong beer an wi wine,
 Untill he was as beastly drunk
  As ony wild-wood swine:
 She's stown the keys o her father's yates
  An latten her true-love in.

8 Whan night was gane, an day was come,
  An the sun shone on their feet,
 Then out it spake him Brown Robin,
  I'll be discoverd yet.

9 Then out it spake that gay lady:
  My love, ye need na doubt;
 For wi ae wile I've got you in,
  Wi anither I'll bring you out.

10 She's taen her to her father's cellar,
  As fast as she can fare;

She's drawn a cup o the gude red wine,
   Hung't low down by her gare;
An she met wi her father dear
   Just coming down the stair.

'I woud na gi that cup, daughter,   11
   That ye hold i your han
For a' the wines in my cellar,
   An gantrees whare the stan.'

'O wae be to your wine, father,   12
   That ever't came oer the sea;
'T'is pitten my head in sick a steer
   I my bowr I canna be.'

'Gang out, gang out, my daughter dear,   13
   Gang out an tack the air;
Gang out an walk i the good green wood,
   An a' your marys fair.'

Then out it spake the proud porter –   14
   Our lady wishd him shame –
'We'll send the marys to the wood,
   But we'll keep our lady at hame.'

'There's thirty marys i my bowr,   15
   There's thirty o them an three;
But there's nae ane amo them a'
   Kens what flowr gains for me.'

She's doen her to her bigly bowr,   16
   As fast as she could gang,
An she has dresst him Brown Robin
   Like ony bowr-woman.

The gown she pat upon her love   17
   Was o the dainty green,
His hose was o the saft, saft silk,
   His shoon o the cordwain fine.

She's pitten his bow in her bosom,   18
   His arrow in her sleeve,
His sturdy bran her body next,
   Because he was her love.

19   Then she is unto her bowr-door,
          As fast as she coud gang;
      But out it spake the proud porter –
          Our lady wishd him shame –
      'We'll count our marys to the wood,
          An we'll count them back again.'

20   The firsten mary she sent out
          Was Brown Robin by name;
      Then out it spake the king himsel.
          'This is a sturdy dame.'

21   O she went out in a May morning,
          In a May morning so gay,
      But she came never back again,
          Her auld father to see.

[Ch 99A]   19. Johnie Scot

1   O Johney was as brave a knight
          As ever saild the sea,
      An he's done him to the English court,
          To serve for meat and fee.

2   He had nae been in fair England
          But yet a little while,
      Untill the kingis ae daughter
          To Johney proves wi chil.

3   O word's come to the king himsel,
          In his chair where he sat,
      That his ae daughter was wi bairn
          To Jack, the Little Scott.

4   'Gin this be true that I do hear,
          As I trust well it be,
      Ye pit her into prison strong,
          An starve her till she die.'

O Johney's on to fair Scotland,   5
    A wot he went wi speed,
An he has left the kingis court,
    A wot good was his need.

O it fell once upon a day   6
    That Johney he thought lang,
An he's gane to the good green wood,
    As fast as he coud gang.

'O whare will I get a bonny boy,   7
    To rin my errand soon,
That will rin into fair England,
    An haste him back again?'

O up it starts a bonny boy,   8
    Gold yallow was his hair,
I wish his mither meickle joy,
    His bonny love mieckle mair.

'O here am I, a bonny boy,   9
    Will rin your errand soon
I will gang into fair England,
    An come right soon again.'

O whan he came to broken briggs,   10
    He bent his bow and swam;
An whan he came to the green grass growan,
    He slaikid his shoone an ran.

Whan he came to yon high castel,   11
    He ran it roun about,
An there he saw the king's daughter,
    At the window looking out.

'O here's a sark o silk, lady,   12
    Your ain han sewd the sleeve;
You'r bidden come to fair Scotlan,
    Speer nane o your parents leave.

'Ha, take this sark o silk, lady,   13
    Your ain han sewd the gare;
You're bidden come to good green wood,
    Love Johney waits you there.'

14   She's turnd her right and roun about,
          The tear was in her ee:
      'How can I come to my true-love,
          Except I had wings to flee?

15   'Here am I kept wi bars and bolts,
          Most grievous to behold;
      My breast-plate's o the sturdy steel,
          Instead of the beaten gold.

16   'But tak this purse, my bonny boy,
          Ye well deserve a fee,
      An bear this letter to my love,
          An tell him what you see.'

17   Then quickly ran the bonny boy
          Again to Scotlan fair,
      An soon he reachd Pitnachton's towrs,
          An soon found Johney there.

18   He pat the letter in his han
          An taul him what he sa,
      But eer he half the letter read,
          He loote the tears down fa.

19   'O I will gae back to fair Englan,
          Tho death shoud me betide,
      An I will relieve the damesel
          That lay last by my side.'

20   Then out it spake his father dear,
          My son, you are to blame;
      An gin you'r catchd on English groun,
          I fear you'll neer win hame.

21   Then out it spake a valiant knight,
          Johny's best friend was he;
      I can commaun five hunder men,
          An I'll his surety be.

22   The firstin town that they came till,
          They gard the bells be rung;
      An the nextin town that they came till,
          They gard the mess be sung.

The thirdin town that they came till,   23
   They gard the drums beat roun;
The king but an his nobles a'
   Was startld at the soun.

Whan they came to the king's palace   24
   They rade it roun about,
An there they saw the king himsel,
   At the window looking out.

'Is this the Duke o Albany,   25
   Or James, the Scottish king?
Or are ye some great foreign lord,
   That's come a visiting?'

'I'm nae the Duke of Albany,   26
   Nor James, the Scottish king;
But I'm a valiant Scottish knight,
   Pitnachton is my name.'

'O if Pitnachton be your name,   27
   As I trust well it be,
The morn, or I tast meat or drink,
   You shall be hanged hi.'

Then out it spake the valiant knight   28
   That came brave Johney wi;
Behold five hunder bowmen bold,
   Will die to set him free.

Then out it spake the king again,   29
   An a scornfu laugh laugh he;
I have an Italian i my house
   Will fight you three by three.

'O grant me a boon,' brave Johney cried;   30
   'Bring your Italian here;
Then if he fall beneath my sword,
   I've won your daughter dear.'

Then out it came that Italian,   31
   An a gurious ghost was he;
Upo the point o Johney's sword
   This Italian did die.

32   Out has he drawn his lang, lang bran,
            Struck it across the plain:
        'Is there any more o your English dogs
            That you want to be slain?'

33   'A clark, a clark,' the king then cried,
            'To write her tocher free;'
        'A priest, a priest,' says Love Johney,
            'To marry my love and me.

34   'I'm seeking nane o your gold,' he says,
            'Nor of your silver clear;
        I only seek your daughter fair,
            Whose love has cost her dear.'

[*Ch 101A*]   20.   Willie o Douglas Dale

1   O Willy was as brave a lord
            As ever saild the sea,
        And he has gane to the English court,
            To serve for meat and fee.

2   He had nae been at the kingis court
            A twelvemonth and a day,
        Till he longd for a sight o the king's daughter,
            But ane he coud never see.

3   O it fell ance upon a day
            To the green wood she has gane,
        An Willy he has followd her,
            With the clear light o the moon.

4   He looted him low, by her did go,
            Wi his hat intill his hand:
        'O what's your will wi me, Sir Knight?
            I pray keep your hat on.'

5   'O I am not a knight, Madam,
            Nor never thinks to be;
        For I am Willy o Douglassdale,
            An I serve for meat and fee.'

'O I'll gang to my bowr,' she says,   6
   'An sigh baith even an morn
That ever I saw your face, Willy,
   Or that ever ye was born.

'O I'll gang to my bowr,' she says,   7
   'An I'll pray baith night an day,
To keep me frae your tempting looks,
   An frae your great beauty.'

O in a little after that   8
   He keepit Dame Oliphant's bowr,
An the love that passd between this twa,
   It was like paramour.

'O narrow, narrow's my gown, Willy,   9
   That wont to be sae wide;
An short, short is my coats, Willy,
   That wont to be sae side;
An gane is a' my fair colour,
   An low laid is my pride.

'But an my father get word of this,   10
   He'll never drink again;
An gin my mother get word of this,
   In her ain bowr she'll go brain;
An gin my bold brothers get word o this,
   I fear, Willy, you'll be slain.'

'O will you leave your father's court,   11
   An go along wi me?
I'll carry you unto fair Scotland,
   And mak you a lady free.'

She pat her han in her pocket   12
   An gae him five hunder poun:
'An take you that now, Squire Willy,
   Till awa that we do won.'

Whan day was gane, and night was come,   13
   She lap the castle-wa;
But Willy kepit his gay lady,
   He was laith to let her fa.

14   Whan night was gane, an day come in,
        An lions gaed to their dens,
    An ay the lady followd him,
        An the tears came hailing down.

15   'O want ye ribbons to your hair?
        Or roses to your shoone?
    Or want ye as meickle dear bought love
        As your ain heart can contain?'

16   'I want nae ribbons to my hair,
        Nor roses till my shoone;
    An Ohone, alas, for dear bought love!
        I have mair nor I can contain.'

17   O he's pu'd the oak in good green wood,
        An he's made to her a fire;
    He coverd it oer wi withred leaves,
        An gard it burn thro ire.

18   He made a bed i the good green wood,
        An he's laid his lady down,
    An he's coverd her oer wi fig-tree leaves,
        But an his ain night-gown.

19   'O had I a bunch o yon red roddins,
        That grows in yonder wood,
    But an a drink o water clear,
        I think it woud do me good.'

20   He's pu'd her a bunch o yon red roddins,
        That grew beside yon thorn,
    But an a drink o water clear,
        Intill his hunting-horn.

21   He's bent his bow, and shot the deer,
        An thro the green wood gane,
    An ere that he came back again
        His lady took travailing.

22   'O up ye tak that horn,' she says,
        'An ye blaw a blast for me;
    Gin my father be in good green wood,
        Sae seen's he'll come me ti.'

'O gin there be a man on earth   23
   That ye loo better nor me,
Ye blaw the horn yoursel,' he says,
   'For it's never be blawn by me.'

O he's bent his bow, an shot the deer,   24
   An thro the green wood has he gane,
An lang or he came back again
   His lady bare him a son.

O up has he tane his bonny young son,   25
   An washn him wi the milk,
An up has he tane his gay lady,
   An rowd her i the silk.

He's bent his bow, and shot the deer,   26
   An thro the green wood has he gane,
Till he met wi a well-fard may,
   Her father's flock feeding.

'Ye leave your father's flock feeding,   27
   An go along wi me;
I'll carry you to a lady fair,
   Will gi you both meat and fee.'

O whan she came the lady before,   28
   She's fa'n down on her knee:
'O what's your will wi me, my dame?
   An a dame you seem to be.'

'O I'm Dame Oliphant, the king's daughter,   29
   Nae doubt but ye've heard o me;
Will you leave your father's flock feeding,
   An go to Scotlan wi me?

'An ye sal get a nouriship   30
   Intill an earldome,
An I will gar provide for the
   To marry some brave Scotsman.'

The may she keepit the bonny boy,   31
   An Willy led his lady,
Untill they took their fair shippin,
   Then quikly hame came they.

32   The win was fair, an the sea was clear,
    An they a' wan safe to lan;
   He's haild her lady of Douglassdale,
    Himsel the lord within.

[Ch 103A] 21. Rose the Red and White Lily

1   O Rose the Red and White Lilly,
    Their mother dear was dead,
   And their father married an ill woman,
    Wishd them twa little guede.

2   Yet she had twa as fu fair sons
    As eer brake manis bread,
   And the tane of them loed her White Lilly,
    An the tither lood Rose the Red.

3   O biggit ha they a bigly bowr,
    And strawn it oer wi san,
   And there was mair mirth i the ladies' bowr
    Than in a' their father's lan.

4   But out it spake their step-mother,
    Wha stood a little foreby:
   I hope to live and play the prank
    Sal gar your loud sang ly.

5   She's calld upon her eldest son:
    Come here, my son, to me;
   It fears me sair, my eldest son,
    That ye maun sail the sea.

6   'Gin it fear you sair, my mither dear,
    Your bidding I maun dee;
   But be never war to Rose the Red
    Than ye ha been to me.'

'O had your tongue, my eldest son,   7
    For sma sal be her part;
You'll nae get a kiss o her comely mouth
    Gin your very fair heart should break.'

She's calld upon her youngest son: 8
    Come here, my son, to me;
It fears me sair, my youngest son,
    That ye maun sail the sea.

'Gin it fear you sair, my mither dear,   9
    Your bidding I maun dee;
But be never war to White Lilly
    Than ye ha been to me.

'O haud your tongue, my youngest son,   10
    For sma sall be her part;
You'll neer get a kiss o her comely mouth
    Tho your very fair heart should break.'

When Rose the Red and White Lilly   11
    Saw their twa loves were gane,
Then stopped ha they their loud, loud sang,
    And tane up the still mournin;
And their step-mother stood listnin by,
    To hear the ladies' mean.

Then out it spake her White Lilly;   12
    My sister, we'll be gane;
Why should we stay in Barnsdale,
    To waste our youth in pain?

Then cutted ha they their green cloathing   13
    A little below their knee,
An sae ha they there yallow hair,
    A little aboon there bree;
An they've doen them to haely chapel,
    Was christened by Our Lady.

There ha they chang'd their ain twa names,   14
    Sae far frae ony town,
An the tane o them hight Sweet Willy,
    An the tither o them Roge the Roun.

15   Between this twa a vow was made,
          An they sware it to fulfil;
      That at three blasts o a bugle-horn,
          She'd come her sister till.

16   Now Sweet Willy's gane to the kingis court,
          Her true-love for to see,
      An Roge the Roun to good green wood,
          Brown Robin's man to be.

17   As it fell out upon a day
          They a' did put the stane,
      Full seven foot ayont them a'
          She gard the puttin-stane gang.

18   She leand her back against an oak,
          And gae a loud Ohone!
      Then out it spake him Brown Robin,
          But that's a woman's moan!

19   'O ken ye by my red rose lip?
          Or by my yallow hair?
      Or ken ye by my milk-white breast?
          For ye never saw it bare?'

20   'I ken no by your red rose lip,
          Nor by your yallow hair;
      Nor ken I by your milk-white breast,
          For I never saw it bare;
      But come to your bowr whaever sae likes,
          Will find a lady there.'

21   'O gin ye come to my bowr within,
          Thro fraud, deceit, or guile,
      Wi this same bran that's in my han,
          I swear I will the kill.'

22   'But I will come thy bowr within,
          An spear nae leave,' quoth he;
      'An this same bran that's i my han
          I sall ware back on the.'

23   About the tenth hour of the night
          The ladie's bower-door was broken,
      An eer the first hour of the day
          The bonny knave-bairn was gotten.

75

When days were gane, and months were run,   24
   The lady took travailing,
And sair she cry'd for a bowr-woman,
   For to wait her upon.

Then out it spake him Brown Robin: 25
   Now what needs a' this din?
For what coud any woman do
   But I coud do the same?

'Twas never my mither's fashion,' she says,   26
   'Nor sall it ever be mine,
That belted knights shoud eer remain
   Where ladies dreed their pine.

'But ye take up that bugle-horn,   27
   An blaw a blast for me;
I ha a brother i the kingis court
   Will come me quickly ti.'

'O gin ye ha a brither on earth   28
   That ye love better nor me,
Ye blaw the horn yoursel,' he says,
   'For ae blast I winna gie.'

She's set the horn till her mouth,   29
   And she's blawn three blasts sae shrill;
Sweet Willy heard i the kingis court,
   And came her quickly till.

Then up it started Brown Robin,   30
   An an angry man was he:
'There comes nae man this bowr within
   But first must fight wi me.'

O they hae fought that bowr within   31
   Till the sun was gaing down,
Till drops o blude frae Rose the Red
   Came hailing to the groun.

She leand her back against the wa,   32
   Says, Robin, let a' be;
For it is a lady born and bred
   That's foughten sae well wi thee.

33 O seven foot he lap a back;
    Says, Alas, and wae is me!
I never wisht in a' my life,
    A woman's blude to see;
An a' for the sake of ae fair maid
    Whose name was White Lilly.

34 Then out it spake her White Lilly,
    An a hearty laugh laugh she:
She's lived wi you this year an mair,
    Tho ye kentna it was she.

35 Now word has gane thro a' the lan,
    Before a month was done,
That Brown Robin's man, in good green wood,
    Had born a bonny young son.

36 The word has gane to the kingis court,
    An to the king himsel;
'Now, by my fay,' the king could say,
    'The like was never heard tell!'

37 Then out it spake him Bold Arthur,
    An a hearty laugh laugh he:
I trow some may has playd the loun,
    And fled her ain country.

38 'Bring me my steed,' then cry'd the king,
    'My bow and arrows keen;
I'l ride mysel to good green wood,
    An see what's to be seen.'

39 'An't please your grace,' said Bold Arthur,
    'My liege, I'll gang you wi,
An try to fin a little foot-page,
    That's strayd awa frae me.'

40 O they've hunted i the good green wood
    The buck but an the rae,
An they drew near Brown Robin's bowr,
    About the close of day.

41 Then out it spake the king in hast,
    Says, Arthur, look an see
Gin that be no your little foot-page
    That leans against yon tree.

Then Arthur took his bugle-horn, 42
    An blew a blast sae shrill;
Sweet Willy started at the sound,
    An ran him quickly till.

'O wanted ye your meat, Willy? 43
    Or wanted ye your fee?
Or gat ye ever an angry word,
    That ye ran awa frae me?'

'I wanted nought, my master dear; 44
    To me ye ay was good;
I came but to see my ae brother,
    That wons in this green wood.'

Then out it spake the king again, 45
    Says, Bonny boy, tell to me
Wha lives into yon bigly bowr,
    Stands by yon green oak tree?

'O pardon me,' says Sweet Willy, 46
    'My liege, I dare no tell;
An I pray you go no near that bowr,
    For fear they do you fell.'

'O haud your tongue, my bonny boy, 47
    For I winna be said nay;
But I will gang that bowr within,
    Betide me weel or wae.'

They've lighted off their milk-white steeds, 48
    An saftly enterd in,
An there they saw her White Lilly,
    Nursing her bonny yong son.

'Now, by the rood,' the king coud say, 49
    'This is a comely sight;
I trow, instead of a forrester's man,
    This is a lady bright!'

Then out it spake her Rose the Red, 50
    An fell low down on her knee:
O pardon us, my gracious liege,
    An our story I'll tell thee.

51   Our father was a wealthy lord,
          That wond in Barnsdale;
      But we had a wicked step-mother,
          That wrought us meickle bale.

52   Yet she had twa as fu fair sons
          As ever the sun did see,
      An the tane o them lood my sister dear,
          An the tither sayd he lood me.

53   Then out it spake him Bold Arthur,
          As by the king he stood:
      Now, by the faith o my body,
          This shoud be Rose the Red!

54   Then in it came him Brown Robin,
          Frae hunting o the deer,
      But whan he saw the king was there,
          He started back for fear.

55   The king has taen him by the hand,
          An bade him naithing dread;
      Says, Ye maun leave the good green wood,
          Come to the court wi speed.

56   Then up he took White Lilly's son,
          An set him on his knee;
      Says, Gin ye live to wiald a bran,
          My bowman ye sall bee.

57   The king he sent for robes of green,
          An girdles o shinning gold;
      He gart the ladies be arrayd
          Most comely to behold.

58   They've done them unto Mary Kirk,
          An there gat fair wedding,
      An fan the news spread oer the lan,
          For joy the bells did ring.

59   Then out it spake her Rose the Red,
          An a hearty laugh laugh she:
      I wonder what would our step-dame say,
          Gin she this sight did see!

22. Sir Hugh [Ch 155A]

Four and twenty bonny boys   1
    Were playing at the ba,
And by it came him sweet Sir Hugh,
    And he playd oer them a'.

He kickd the ba with his right foot,   2
    And catchd it wi his knee,
And throuch-and-thro the Jew's window
    He gard the bonny ba flee.

He's doen him to the Jew's castell,   3
    And walkd it round about;
And there he saw the Jew's daughter,
    At the window looking out.

'Throw down the ba, ye Jew's daughter,   4
    Throw down the ba to me!'
'Never a bit,' says the Jew's daughter,
    'Till up to me come ye.'

'How will I come up? How can I come up?   5
    How can I come to thee?
For as ye did to my auld father,
    The same ye'll do to me.'

She's gane till her father's garden,   6
    And pu'd an apple red and green;
'T was a' to wyle him sweet Sir Hugh,
    And to entice him in.

She's led him in through ae dark door,   7
    And sae has she thro nine;
She's laid him on a dressing-table,
    And stickit him like a swine.

And first came out the thick, thick blood,   8
    And syne came out the thin,
And syne came out the bonny heart's blood;
    There was nae mair within.

She's rowd him in a cake o lead,   9
    Bade him lie still and sleep;
She's thrown him in Our Lady's draw-well,
    Was fifty fathom deep.

10   When bells were rung, and mass was sung,
        And a' the bairns came hame,
     When every lady gat hame her son,
        The Lady Maisry gat nane.

11   She's taen her mantle her about,
        Her coffer by the hand,
     And she's gane out to seek her son,
        And wanderd oer the land.

12   She's doen her to the Jew's castell,
        Where a' were fast asleep:
     'Gin ye be there, my sweet Sir Hugh,
        I pray you to me speak.'

13   She's doen her to the Jew's garden,
        Thought he had been gathering fruit:
     'Gin ye be there, my sweet Sir Hugh,
        I pray you to me speak.'

14   She neard Our Lady's deep draw-well,
        Was fifty fathom deep:
     'Whareer ye be, my sweet Sir Hugh,
        I pray you to me speak.'

15   'Gae hame, gae hame, my mither dear,
        Prepare my winding sheet,
     And at the back o merry Lincoln
        The morn I will you meet.'

16   Now Lady Maisry is gane hame,
        Made him a winding sheet,
     And at the back o merry Lincoln
        The dead corpse did her meet.

17   And a' the bells o merry Lincoln
        Without men's hands were rung,
     And a' the books o merry Lincoln
        Were read without man's tongue,
     And neer was such a burial
        Sin Adam's days begun.

23. The Baron of Brackley   [*Ch 203C*]

O Inverey came down Dee side, whistling and playing;   1
He's landed at Braikly's yates at the day dawing.

Says, Baron of Braikly, are ye within?   2
There's sharp swords at the yate will gar your blood spin.

The lady raise up, to the window she went;   3
She heard her kye lowing oer hill and oer bent.

'O rise up, John,' she says, 'turn back your kye;   4
They're oer the hills rinning, they're skipping away.'

'Come to your bed, Peggie, and let the kye rin,   5
For were I to gang out, I would never get in.'

Then she's cry'd on her women, they quickly came ben: 6
'Take up your rocks, lassies, and fight a' like men.

'Though I'm but a woman, to head you I'll try,   7
Nor let these vile Highland-men steal a' our kye.'

Then up gat the baron, and cry'd for his graith;   8
Says, Lady, I'll gang, tho to leave you I'm laith.

'Come, kiss me, my Peggie, nor think I'm to blame;   9
For I may well gang out, but I'll never win in.'

When the Baron of Braikly rade through the close,   10
A gallanter baron neer mounted a horse.

Tho there came wi Inverey thirty and three,   11
There was nane wi bonny Braikly but his brother and he.

Twa gallanter Gordons did never sword draw;   12
But against four and thirty, wae's me, what was twa?

Wi swords and wi daggers they did him surround,   13
And they've pierc'd bonny Braikly wi mony a wound.

Frae the head of the Dee to the banks of the Spey,   14
The Gordons may mourn him, and bann Inverey.

'O came ye by Braikly, and was ye in there?   15
Or saw ye his Peggy dear riving her hair?'

'O I came by Braikly, and I was in there,   16
But I saw not his Peggy dear riving her hair.'

17   'O fye on ye, lady! how could ye do sae?
        You opend your yate to the faus Inverey.'

18   She eat wi him, drank wi him, welcomd him in;
        She welcomd the villain that slew her baron.

19   She kept him till morning, syne bad him be gane,
        And showd him the road that he woud na be tane.

20   'Thro Birss and Aboyne,' she says, 'lyin in a tour,
        Oer the hills of Glentanor you'll skip in an hour.'

21   There is grief in the kitchen, and mirth in the ha,
        But the Baron of Braikly is dead and awa.

[*Ch 222A*]   24. Bonny Baby Livingston

1   O Bonny Baby Livingston
            Went forth to view the hay,
        And by it came him Glenlion,
            Sta bonny Baby away.

2   O first he's taen her silken coat,
            And neest her satten gown,
        Syne rowd her in a tartan plaid,
            And hapd her round and rown.

3   He has set her upon his steed
            And roundly rode away,
        And neer loot her look back again
            The live-long summer's day.

4   He's carried her oer hills and muirs
            Till they came to a Highland glen,
        And there he's met his brother John,
            With twenty armed men.

5   O there were cows, and there were ewes,
            And lasses milking there,
        But Baby neer anse lookd about,
            Her heart was filld wi care.

Glenlion took her in his arms,   6
   And kissd her, cheek and chin;
Says, I'd gie a' these cows and ewes
   But ae kind look to win.

'O ae kind look ye neer shall get,   7
   Nor win a smile frae me,
Unless to me you'll favour shew,
   And take me to Dundee.'

'Dundee, Baby? Dundee, Baby?   8
   Dundee you neer shall see
Till I've carried you to Glenlion
   And have my bride made thee.

'We'll stay a while at Auchingour,   9
   And get sweet milk and cheese,
And syne we'll gang to Glenlion,
   And there live at our ease.'

'I winna stay at Auchingour,   10
   Nor eat sweet milk and cheese,
Nor go with thee to Glenlion,
   For there I'll neer find ease.'

Than out it spake his brother John,   11
   'O were I in your place,
I'd take that lady hame again,
   For a' her bonny face.

'Commend me to the lass that's kind,   12
   Tho na so gently born;
And, gin her heart I coudna gain,
   To take her hand I'd scorn.'

'O had your tongue now, John,' he says,   13
   'You wis na what you say;
For I've lood that bonny face
   This twelve month and a day.

'And tho I've lood her lang and sair   14
   A smile I neer coud win;
Yet what I've got anse in my power
   To keep I think nae sin.'

15   When they came to Glenlion castle,
         They lighted at the yate,
     And out it came his sisters three,
         Wha did them kindly greet.

16   O they've taen Baby by the hands
         And led her oer the green,
     And ilka lady spake a word,
         But bonny Baby spake nane.

17   Then out it spake her bonny Jean,
         The youngest o the three,
     'O lady, dinna look sae sad,
         But tell your grief to me.'

18   'O wherefore should I tell my grief,
         Since lax I canna find?
     I'm stown frae a' my kin and friends,
         And my love I left behind.

19   'But had I paper, pen, and ink,
         Before that it were day,
     I yet might get a letter sent
         In time to Johny Hay.'

20   O she's got paper, pen, and ink,
         And candle that she might see,
     And she has written a broad letter
         To Johny at Dundee.

21   And she has gotten a bonny boy,
         That was baith swift and strang,
     Wi philabeg and bonnet blue,
         Her errand for to gang.

22   'O boy, gin ye'd my blessing win
         And help me in my need,
     Run wi this letter to my love,
         And bid him come wi speed.

23   'And here's a chain of good red gowd,
         And gowdn guineas three,
     And when you've well your errand done,
         You'll get them for your fee.

The boy he ran oer hill and dale,   24
   Fast as a bird coud flee,
And eer the sun was twa hours height
   The boy was at Dundee.

And when he came to Johny's door   25
   He knocked loud and sair;
Then Johny to the window came,
   And loudly cry'd, 'Wha's there?'

'O here's a letter I have brought,   26
   Which ye maun quickly read,
And, gin ye woud your lady save,
   Gang back wi me wi speed.'

O when he had the letter read,   27
   An angry man was he;
He says, Glenlion, thou shalt rue
   This deed of villany!

'O saddle to me the black, the black,   28
   O saddle to me the brown,
O saddle to me the swiftest steed
   That eer rade frae the town.

'And arm ye well, my merry men a',   29
   And follow me to the glen,
For I vow I'll neither eat nor sleep
   Till I get my love again.'

He's mounted on a milk-white steed,   30
   The boy upon a gray,
And they got to Glenlion's castle
   About the close of day.

As Baby at her window stood,   31
   The west wind saft did bla;
She heard her Johny's well-kent voice
   Beneath the castle wa.

'O Baby, haste, the window jump!   32
   I'll kep you in my arm;
My merry men a' are at the yate,
   To rescue you frae harm.'

33   She to the window fixt her sheets
         And slipped safely down,
      And Johny catchd her in his arms,
         Neer loot her touch the ground.

34   When mounted on her John's horse.
         Fou blithely did she say,
      'Glenlion, you hae lost your bride!
         She's aff wi Johny Hay.'

35   Glenlion and his brother John
         Were birling in the ha,
      When they heard Johny's bridle ring,
         As first he rade awa.

36   'Rise, Jock, gang out and meet the priest,
         I hear his bridle ring;
      My Baby now shall be my wife
         Before the laverocks sing.'

37   'O brother, this is not the priest;
         I fear he'll come oer late;
      For armed men with shining brands
         Stand at the castle-yate.'

38   'Haste Donald, Duncan, Dugald, Hugh!
         Haste, take your sword and spier!
      We'll gar these traytors rue the hour
         That eer they ventured here.'

39   The Highland men drew their claymores,
         And gae a warlike shout,
      But Johny's merry men kept the yate,
         Nae ane durst venture out.

40   The lovers rade the live-lang night,
         And safe gat on their way,
      And bonny Baby Livingston
         Has gotten Johny Hay.

41   'Awa, Glenlion! fy for shame!
         Gae hide ye in some den!
      You've lettn your bride be stown frae you,
         For a' your armed men.'

25. The Kitchie-Boy [Ch 252C]

O there was a ladie, a noble ladie,   1
    She was a ladie of birth and fame,
But she fell in love wi her father's foot-boy,
    I wis she was the mair to blame.

A word of him she neer could get   2
    Till her father was a hunting gone;
Then she calld on the bonny foot-boy
    To speak wi her in her bower alone.

Says, Ye ken you are my love, Willie,   3
    And that I am a ladie free,
And there's naething ye can ask, Willie,
    But at your bidding I maun be.

O the loving looks that ladie gave   4
    Soon made the bonny boy grow bold,
And the loving words that ladie spake
    As soon on them he did lay hold.

She has taen a ring frae her white finger,   5
    And unto him she did it gie;
Says, Wear this token for my sake,
    And keep it till the day you die.

'But shoud my father get word of this   6
    I fear we baith will have cause to rue,
For to some nunnery I shoud be sent,
    And I fear, my love, he would ruin you.

'But here is a coffer of the good red gowd,   7
    I wot my mother left it to me;
And wi it you'll buy a bonny ship,
    And ye maun sail the raging sea;
Then like some earl or baron's son
    You can come back and marrie me.

But stay not lang awa, Willie,   8
    O stay not lang across the fame,
For fear your ladie shoud lighter be,
    Or your young son shoud want a name.'

9   He had not been o the sea sailling
           But till three months were come and gane,
      Till he has landed his bonny ship;
           It was upon the coast of Spain.

10   There was a ladie of high degree
           That saw him walking up and down;
      She fell in love wi sweet Willie,
           But she wist no how to make it known.

11   She has calld up her maries a',
           Says, Hearken well to what I say;
      There is a young man in yon ship
           That has been my love this many a day.

12   'Now bear a hand, my maries a',
           And busk me brave and make me fine,
      And go wi me to yon shore-side
           To invite that noble youth to dine.'

13   O they have buskit that ladie gay
           In velvet pall and jewels rare;
      A poor man might have been made rich
           Wi half the pearles they pat in her hair.

14   Her mantle was of gowd sae red,
           It glaned as far as ane coud see;
      Sweet Willie thought she had been the queen,
           And bowd full low and bent his knee.

15   She's gard her maries step aside,
           And on sweet Willie sae did smile;
      She thought that man was not on earth
           But of his heart she could beguile.

16   Says, Ye maun leave your bonny ship
           And go this day wi me and dine,
      And you shall eat the baken meat,
           And you shall drink the Spanish wine.

17   'I canna leave my bonny ship,
           Nor go this day to dine wi thee,
      For a' my sails are ready bent
           To bear me back to my ain countrie.'

'O gin you'd forsake your bonny ship 18
    And wed a ladie of this countrie,
I would make you lord of a' this town,
    And towns and castles twa or three.'

'Should I wed a ladie of this countrie, 19
    In sooth I woud be sair to blame,
For the fairest ladie in fair Scotland
    Woud break her heart gin I gaed na hame.'

'That ladie may choose another lord, 20
    And you another love may choose;
There is not a lord in this countrie
    That such a proffer could refuse.'

'O ladie, shoud I your proffer take, 21
    You'd soon yoursell have cause to rue,
For the man that his first love forsakes
    Woud to a seccond neer prove true.'

She has taen a ring frae her white finger, 22
    It might have been a prince's fee;
Says, Wear this token for my sake,
    And give me that which now I see.

'Take back your token, ye ladie fair; 23
    This ring you see on my right hand
Was gien me by my ain true-love,
    Before I left my native land.

'And tho yours woud buy it nine times oer 24
    I far more dearly prize my ain;
Nor woud I make the niffer,' he says,
    'For a' the gowd that is in Spain.'

The ladie turnd her head away 25
    To dry the sat tears frae her eyne;
She naething more to him did say
    But, I wish your face I neer had seen!

He has set his foot on good ship-board, 26
    The ladie waved her milk-white hand,
The wind sprang up and filld his sails,
    And he quickly left the Spanish land.

27   He soon came back to his native strand,
            He langd his ain true-love to see;
        Her father saw him come to land,
            And took him some great lord to be.

28   Says, Will ye leave your bonny ship
            And come wi me this day to dine?
        And you shall eat the baken meat,
            And you shall drink the claret wine.

29   'O I will leave my bonny ship,
            And gladly go wi you to dine,
        And I woud gie thrice three thousand pounds
            That your fair daughter were but mine.'

30   'O gin ye will part wi your bonny ship
            And wed a ladie of this countrie,
        I will gie you my ae daughter,
            Gin she'll consent your bride to be.'

31   O he has blaket his bonny face
            And closs tuckd up his yellow hair;
        His true-love met them at the yate,
            But she little thought her love was there.

32   'O will you marrie this lord, daughter,
            That I've brought hame to dine wi me?
        You shall be heir of a' my lands,
            Gin you'll consent his bride to be.'

33   She looked oer her left shoulder,
            I wot the tears stood in her eye;
        Says, The man is on the sea sailling
            That fair wedding shall get of me.

34   Then Willie has washd his bonny face,
            And he's kaimd down his yellow hair;
        He took his true-love in his arms,
            And kindly has he kissd her there.

35   She's looked in his bonny face,
            And thro her tears did sweetly smile,
        Then sayd, Awa, awa, Willie!
            How could you thus your love beguile?

She kept the secret in her breast,   36
   Full seven years she's kept the same,
Till it fell out at a christning-feast,
   And then of it she made good game.

And her father laughd aboon the rest,   37
   And said, My daughter, you'r nae to blame;
For you've married for love, and no for land,
   So a' my gowd is yours to claim.

The Tradition
in Transition: The Ballads
of James Nicol

[Ch 34A]   26. Kemp Owyne

1   Her mother died when she was young,
        Which gave her cause to make great moan;
    Her father married the warst woman
        That ever lived in Christendom.

2   She served her with foot and hand,
        In every thing that she could dee,
    Till once, in an unlucky time,
        She threw her in ower Craigy's sea.

3   Says, 'Lie you there, dove Isabel,
        And all my sorrows lie with thee;
    Till Kemp Owyne come ower the sea,
        And borrow you with kisses three,
    Let all the warld do what they will,
        Oh borrowed shall you never be!'

4   Her breath grew strang, her hair grew lang,
        And twisted thrice about the tree,
    And all the people, far and near,
        Thought that a savage beast was she.

5   These news did come to Kemp Owyne,
        Where he lived, far beyond the sea;
    He hasted him to Craigy's sea,
        And on the savage beast lookd he.

6   Her breath was strang, her hair was lang,
        And twisted was about the tree,
    And with a swing she came about:
        'Come to Craigy's sea, and kiss with me.

7   'Here is a royal belt,' she cried,
        'That I have found in the green sea;
    And while your body it is on,
        Drawn shall your blood never be;
    But if you touch me, tail or fin,
        I vow my belt your death shall be.'

He stepped in, gave her a kiss,   8
   The royal belt he brought him wi;
Her breath was strang, her hair was lang,
   And twisted twice about the tree,
And with a swing she came about:
   'Come to Craigy's sea, and kiss with me.

'Here is a royal ring,' she said,   9
   'That I have found in the green sea;
And while your finger it is on,
   Drawn shall your blood never be;
But if you touch me, tail or fin,
   I swear my ring your death shall be.'

He stepped in, gave her a kiss,   10
   The royal ring he brought him wi;
Her breath was strang, her hair was lang,
   And twisted ance about the tree,
And with a swing she came about:
   'Come to Craigy's sea, and kiss with me.

'Here is a royal brand,' she said,   11
   'That I have found in the green sea;
And while your body it is on,
   Drawn shall your blood never be;
But if you touch me, tail or fin,
   I swear my brand your death shall be.'

He stepped in, gave her a kiss,   12
   The royal brand he brought him wi;
Her breath was sweet, her hair grew short,
   And twisted nane about the tree,
And smilingly she came about,
   As fair a woman as fair could be.

1   O all you ladies young and gay,
         Who are so sweet and fair,
     Do not go into Chaster's wood,
         For Tomlin will be there.

2   Fair Margret sat in her bonny bower,
         Sewing her silken seam,
     And wished to be in Chaster's wood,
         Among the leaves so green.

3   She let her seam fall to her foot,
         The needle to her toe,
     And she has gone to Chaster's wood,
         As fast as she could go.

4   When she began to pull the flowers,
         She pulld both red and green;
     Then by did come, and by did go,
         Said, Fair maid, let aleene.

5   'O why pluck you the flowers, lady,
         Or why climb you the tree?
     Or why come ye to Chaster's wood
         Without the leave of me?'

6   'O I will pull the flowers,' she said,
         'Or I will break the tree,
     For Chaster's wood it is my own,
         I'll no ask leave at thee.'

7   He took her by the milk-white hand,
         And by the grass green sleeve,
     And laid her low down on the flowers,
         At her he asked no leave.

8   The lady blushed, and sourly frowned,
         And she did think great shame;
     Says, 'If you are a gentleman,
         You will tell me your name.'

9   'First they did call me Jack,' he said,
         'And then they called me John,
     But since I lived in the fairy court
         Tomlin has always been my name.

97

'So do not pluck that flower, lady,   10
    That has these pimples gray;
They would destroy the bonny babe
    That we've got in our play.'

'O tell me, Tomlin,' she said,   11
    'And tell it to me soon,
Was you ever at good church-door,
    Or got you christendoom?'

'O I have been at good church-door,   12
    And aff her yetts within;
I was the Laird of Foulis's son,
    The heir of all this land.

'But it fell once upon a day,   13
    As hunting I did ride,
As I rode east and west yon hill
    There woe did me betide.

'O drowsy, drowsy as I was!   14
    Dead sleep upon me fell;
The Queen of Fairies she was there,
    And took me to hersell.

'The Elfins is a pretty place,   15
    In which I love to dwell,
But yet at every seven years' end
    The last here goes to hell;
And as I am ane o flesh and blood,
    I fear the next be mysell.

'The morn at even is Halloween;   16
    Our fairy court will ride,
Throw England and Scotland both,
    Throw al the world wide;
And if ye would me borrow,
    At Rides Cross ye may bide.

'You may go into the Miles Moss,   17
    Between twelve hours and one;
Take holy water in your hand,
    And cast a compass round.

18
    'The first court that comes along,
      You'll let them all pass by;
    The next court that comes along,
      Salute them reverently.

19
    'The next court that comes along
      Is clad in robes of green,
    And it's the head court of them all,
      For in it rides the queen.

20
    'And I upon a milk-white steed,
      With a gold star in my crown;
    Because I am an earthly man
      I'm next to the queen in renown.

21
    'Then seize upon me with a spring,
      Then to the ground I'll fa,
    And then you'll hear a rueful cry
      That Tomlin is awa.

22
    'Then I'll grow in your arms two
      Like to a savage wild;
    But hold me fast, let me not go,
      I'm father of your child.

23
    'I'll grow into your arms two
      Like an adder or a snake;
    But hold me fast, let me not go,
      I'll be your earthly maick.

24
    'I'll grow into your arms two
      Like iron in strong fire;
    But hold me fast, let me not go,
      Then you'll have your desire.'

25
    She rid down to Miles Cross,
      Between twelve hours and one,
    Took holy water in her hand,
      And cast a compass round.

26
    The first court that came along,
      She let them all pass by;
    The next court that came along
      Saluted reverently.

The next court that came along   27
  Were clad in robes of green,
When Tomlin, on a milk-white steed,
  She saw ride with the queen.

She seized him in her arms two,   28
  He to the ground did fa,
And then she heard a ruefull cry
  'Tomlin is now awa.'

He grew into her arms two   29
  Like to a savage wild;
She held him fast, let him not go,
  The father of her child.

He grew into her arms two   30
  Like an adder or a snake;
She held him fast, let him not go,
  He was her earthly maick.

He grew into her arms two   31
  Like iron in hot fire;
She held him fast, let him not go,
  He was her heart's desire.

Then sounded out throw elphin court,   32
  With a loud shout and a cry,
That the pretty maid of Chaster's wood
  That day had caught her prey.

'O stay, Tomlin,' cried Elphin Queen,   33
  'Till I pay you your fee;'
'His father has lands and rents enough,
  He wants no fee from thee.'

'O had I known at early morn   34
  Tomlin would from me gone,
I would have taken out his heart of flesh
  Put in a heart of stone.'

1   'O well like I to ride in a mist,
     And shoot in a northern win,
   And far better a lady to steal,
     That's come of a noble kin.'

2   Four an twenty fair ladies
     Put on this lady's sheen,
   And as mony young gentlemen
     Did lead her ower the green.

3   Yet she preferred before them all
     Him, young Hastings the Groom;
   He's coosten a mist before them all,
     And away this lady has taen.

4   He's taken the lady on him behind,
     Spared neither grass nor corn,
   Till they came to the wood o Amonshaw,
     Where again their loves were sworn.

5   And they hae lived in that wood
     Full mony a year and day,
   And were supported from time to time
     By what he made of prey.

6   And seven bairns, fair and fine,
     There she has born to him,
   And never was in gude church-door,
     Nor ever got gude kirking.

7   Ance she took harp into her hand,
     And harped them a' asleep,
   Then she sat down at their couch-side,
     And bitterly did weep.

8   Said, Seven bairns hae I born now
     To my lord in the ha;
   I wish they were seven greedy rats,
     To run upon the wa,
   And I mysel a great grey cat,
     To eat them ane and a'.

For ten lang years now I hae lived 9
    Within this cave of stane,
And never was at gude church-door,
    Nor got no gude churching.

O then out spake her eldest child, 10
    And a fine boy was he:
O hold your tongue, my mother dear;
    I'll tell you what to dee.

Take you the youngest in your lap, 11
    The next youngest by the hand,
Put all the rest of us you before,
    As you learnt us to gang.

And go with us unto some kirk – 12
    You say they are built of stane –
And let us all be christened,
    And you get gude kirking.

She took the youngest in her lap, 13
    The next youngest by the hand,
Set all the rest of them her before,
    As she learnt them to gang.

And she has left the wood with them, 14
    And to the kirk has gane,
Where the gude priest them christened,
    And gave her gude kirking.

29. Lady Maisry   [*Ch 65B*]

In came her sister, 1
    Stepping on the floor;
Says, It's telling me, my sister Janet,
    That you're become a whore.

'A whore, sister, a whore, sister? 2
    That's what I'll never be;
I'm no so great a whore, sister,
    As liars does on me lee.'

3   In came her brother,
        Stepping on the floor;
      Says, It's telling me, my sister Janet,
        That you're become a whore.'

4   'A whore, brother, a whore, brother?
        A whore I'll never be;
      I'm no so bad a woman, brother,
        As liars does on me lee.'

5   In came her mother,
        Stepping on the floor:
      'They are telling me, my daughter,
        That you're so soon become a whore.'

6   'A whore, mother, a whore, mother?
        A whore I'll never be;
      I'm only with child to an English lord,
        Who promised to marry me.'

7   In came her father,
        Stepping on the floor;
      Says, They tell me, my daughter Janet,
        That you are become a whore.'

8   'A whore, father, a whore, father?
        A whore I'll never be;
      I'm but with child to an English lord,
        Who promised to marry me.'

9   Then in it came an old woman,
        The lady's nurse was she,
      And ere she could get out a word
        The tear blinded her ee.

10   'Your father's to the fire, Janet,
        Your brother's to the whin;
      All for to kindle a bold bonfire,
        To burn your body in.'

11   'Where will I get a boy,' she said,
        'Will gain gold for his fee,
      That would run unto fair England
        For my good lord to me?'

'O I have here a boy,' she said,   12
　　'Will gain gold to his fee,
For he will run to fair England
　　For thy good lord to thee.'

Now when he found a bridge broken,   13
　　He bent his bow and swam,
And when he got where grass did grow,
　　He slacked it and ran.

And when he came to that lord's gate,   14
　　Stopt not to knock or call,
But set his bent bow to his breast
　　And lightly leapt the wall;
And ere the porter could open the gate,
　　The boy was in the hall,

In presence of that noble lord,   15
　　And fell down on his knee:
'What is it, my boy,' he cried,
　　'Have you brought unto me?

'Is my building broke into?   16
　　Or is my towers won?
Or is my true-love delivered
　　Of daughter or of son?'

'Your building is not broke,' he cried,   17
　　'Nor is your towers won,
Nor is your true-love delivered
　　Of daughter nor of son;
But if you do not come in haste,
　　Be sure she will be gone.

'Her father is gone to the fire,   18
　　Her brother to the whin,
To kindle up a bold bonfire,
　　To burn her body in.'

'Go saddle to me the black,' he cried,   19
　　'And do it very soon;
Get unto me the swiftest horse
　　That ever rade from the town.'

20   The first horse that he rade upon,
          For he was raven black,
      He bore him far, and very far,
          But failed in a slack.

21   The next horse that he rode upon,
          He was a bonny brown;
      He bore him far, and very far,
          But did at last fall down.

22   The next horse that he rode upon,
          He as the milk was white;
      Fair fall the mare that foaled that foal
          Took him to Janet's sight!

23   And boots and spurs, all as he was,
          Into the fire he lap,
      Got one kiss of her comely mouth,
          While her body gave a crack.

24   'O who has been so bold,' he says,
          'This bonfire to set on?
      Or who has been so bold,' he says,
          'Her body for to burn?'

25   'O here are we,' her brother said,
          'This bonfire who set on;
      And we have been so bold,' he said,
          'Her body for to burn.'

26   'O I'll cause burn for you, Janet,
          Your father and your mother;
      And I'll cause die for you, Janet,
          Your sister and your brother.

27   'And I'll cause mony back be bare,
          And mony shed be thin,
      And mony wife be made a widow,
          And mony ane want their son.'

30. Lord Ingram and [*Ch 66A*] Chiel Wyet

Lord Ingram and Chiel Wyet   1
   Was baith born in one bower;
Laid baith their hearts on one lady,
   The less was their honour.

Chiel Wyet and Lord Ingram   2
   Was baith born in one hall;
Laid baith their hearts on one lady,
   The worse did them befall.

Lord Ingram wood her Lady Maisery   3
   From father and from mother;
Lord Ingram wood her Lady Maisery
   From sister and from brother.

Lord Ingram wood her Lady Maisery   4
   With leave of a' her kin;
And every one gave full consent,
   But she said no to him.

Lord Ingram wood her Lady Maisery   5
   Into her father's ha;
Chiel Wyet wood her Lady Maisery
   Amang the sheets so sma.

Now it fell out upon a day,   6
   She was dressing her head,
That ben did come her father dear,
   Wearing the gold so red.

He said, Get up now, Lady Maisery,   7
   Put on your wedding gown;
For Lord Ingram he will be here,
   Your wedding must be done.

I'd rather be Chiel Wyet's wife,   8
   The white fish for to sell,
Before I were Lord Ingram's wife,
   To wear the silk so well.

9   'I'd rather be Chiel Wyet's wife,
            With him to beg my bread,
        Before I were Lord Ingram's wife,
            To wear the gold so red.

10   'Where will I get a bonny boy,
            Will win gold to his fee,
        And will run unto Chiel Wyet's,
            With this letter from me?'

11   'O here I am,' the boy says
            'Will win gold to my fee,
        And carry away any letter
            To Chiel Wyet from thee.'

12   And when he found the bridges broke,
            He bent his bow and swam;
        And when he found the grass growing,
            He hastened and he ran.

13   And when he came to Chiel Wyet's castle,
            He did not knock or call,
        But set his bent bow to his breast,
            And lightly leaped the wall;
        And ere the porter opend the gate,
            The boy was in the hall.

14   The first line he looked on,
            A grieved man was he;
        The next line he looked on,
            A tear blinded his ee:
        Says, I wonder what ails my one brother
            He'll not let my love be!

15   'But I'll send to my brother's bridal –
            The bacon shall be mine –
        Full four and twenty buck and roe,
            And ten tun of the wine;
        And bid my love be blythe and glad,
            And I will follow syne.'

16   There was not a groom about that castle
            But got a gown of green,
        And all was blythe, and all was glad,
            But Lady Maisery she was neen.

There was no cook about that kitchen　　　　17
　　But got a gown of gray,
And all was blythe, and all was glad,
　　But Lady Maisery was wae.

Between Mary Kirk and that castle　　　　18
　　Was all spread ower with garl,
To keep Lady Maisery and her maidens
　　From tramping on the marl.

From Mary Kirk to that castle　　　　19
　　Was spread a cloth of gold,
To keep Lady Maisery and her maidens
　　From treading on the mold.

When mass was sung, and bells was rung,　　　　20
　　And all men bound for bed,
Then Lord Ingram and Lady Maisery
　　In one bed they were laid.

When they were laid into their bed –　　　　21
　　It was baith saft and warm –
He laid his hand over her side,
　　Says, I think you are with bairn.

'I told you once, so did I twice,　　　　22
　　When ye came me to woo,
That Chiel Wyet, your only brother,
　　One night lay in my bower.

'I told you twice, I told you thrice,　　　　23
　　Ere ye came me to wed,
That Chiel Wyet, your one brother,
　　One night lay in my bed.'

'O will you father your bairn on me,　　　　24
　　And on no other man?
And I'll give him to his dowry
　　Full fifty ploughs of land.'

'I will not father my bairn on you,　　　　25
　　Nor on no wrongeous man,
Though ye would give him to his dowry
　　Five thousand ploughs of land.'

26   Then up did start him Chiel Wyet,
            Shed by his yellow hair,
        And gave Lord Ingram to the heart
            A deep wound and a sair.

27   Then up did start him Lord Ingram,
            Shed by his yellow hair,
        And gave Chiel Wyet to the heart
            A deep wound and a sair.

28   There was no pity for that two lords,
            Where they were lying slain;
        But all was for her Lady Maisery,
            In that bower she gaed brain.

29   There was no pity for that two lords,
            When they were lying dead;
        But all was for her Lady Maisery,
            In that bower she went mad.

30   Said, Get to me a cloak of cloth,
            A staff of good hard tree;
        If I have been an evil woman,
            I shall beg till I dee.

31   'For a bit I'll beg for Chiel Wyet,
            For Lord Ingram I'll beg three;
        All for the good and honorable marriage
            At Mary Kirk he gave me.'

[Ch 72D] 31. The Clerk's Twa Sons o Owsenford

1   Oh I will tell a tale of woe,
            Which makes my heart richt sair;
        The Clerk's two sons of Oxenfoord
            Are too soon gone to lair.

2   They thought their father's service mean,
            Their mother's no great affair;
        But they would go to fair Berwick,
            To learn [some] unco lair.

109

They had not been in fair Berwick   3
   A twelve month and a day,
Till the clerk's two sons of Oxenford
   With the mayor's two daughters lay.

This word came to the mighty mayor,   4
   As he hunted the rae,
That the clerks two sons of Oxenfoord
   With his two daughters lay.

'If they have lain with my daughters,   5
   The heirs of all my land,
I make a vow, and will keep it true,
   To hang them with my hand.'

When he was certain of the fact,   6
   An angry man was he,
And he has taken these two brothers,
   And hanged them on the tree.

Word it has come to Oxenfoord's clerk,   7
   Ere it was many day,
That his two sons sometime ago
   With the mayor's two daughters lay.

'O saddle a horse to me,' he cried,   8
   'O do it quick and soon,
That I may ride to fair Berwick,
   And see what can be done.'

But when he came to fair Berwick   9
   A grieved man was he,
When that he saw his two bonnie sons
   Both hanging on the tree.

'O woe is me,' the clerk cried out,   10
   'This dismal sight to see,
All the whole comfort of my life
   Dead hanging on the tree!'

He turned his horse's head about,   11
   Making a piteous moan,
And all the way to Oxenfoord
   Did sad and grievously groan.

12   His wife did hastily cry out,
                'You only do I see;
            What have you done with my two sons,
                You should have brought to me?'

13   'I put them to some higher lair,
                And to a deeper scule;
            You will not see your bonnie sons
                Till the haly days of Yule.

14   'And I will spend my days in grief,
                Will never laugh nor sing;
            There's never a man in Oxenfoord
                Shall hear my bridle ring.'

[*Ch 110E*]   32. The Knight and
Shepherd's Daughter

1   Earl Richard, once upon a day,
                And all his valiant men so wight,
            He did him down to Barnisdale,
                Where all the land is fair and light.

2   He was aware of a damosel –
                I wot fast on she did her bound –
            With towers of gold upon her head,
                As fair a woman as could be found.

3   He said, Busk on you, fair ladye,
                The white flowers and the red;
            For I would give my bonnie ship
                To get your maidenhead.

4   'I wish your bonnie ship rent and rive,
                And drown you in the sea;
            For all this would not mend the miss
                That ye would do to me.'
            'The miss is not so great, ladye;
                Soon mended it might be.

'I have four an twenty mills in Scotland,   5
    Stands on the water of Tay;
You'll have them, and as much flour
    As they'll grind in a day.'

'I wish your bonnie ship rent and rive,   6
    And drown you in the sea;
For all that would not mend the miss
    That ye would do to me.'
'The miss is not so great, ladye;
    Soon mended it will be.

'I have four and twenty milk-white cows,   7
    All calved in a day;
You'll have them, and as much haind grass
    As they all on can gae.'

'I wish your bonnie ship rent and rive,   8
    And drown you in the sea;
For all that would not mend the miss
    That ye would do to me.'
'The miss is not so great, ladye;
    Soon mended it might be.

'I have four and twenty milk-white steeds,   9
    All foaled in one year;
You'll have them, and as much red gold
    As all their backs can bear.'

She turned her right and round about,   10
    And she swore by the mold;
'I would not be your love,' said she,
    'For that church full of gold.'

He turned him right and round about,   11
    And he swore by the mess;
Says, Ladye, ye my love shall be,
    And gold ye shall have less.

She turned her right and round about,   12
    And she swore by the moon;
'I would not be your love,' says she,
    'For all the gold in Rome.'

13   He turned him right and round about,
            And he swore by the moon;
        Says, Ladye, ye my love shall be,
            And gold ye shall have none.

14   He caught her by the milk-white hand,
            And by the grass-green sleeve,
        And there has taken his will of her,
            Wholly without her leave.

15   The ladye frownd, and sadly blushd,
            And oh, but she thought shame!
        Says, If you are a knight at all,
            You surely will tell me your name.

16   'In some places they call me Jack,
            In other some they call me John;
        But when into the queen's court,
            O then Lithcock it is my name!'

17   'Lithcock! Lithcock!' the ladye said,
            And oft she spelt it ower again;
        'Lithcock! it's Latin,' the ladye said,
            'Richard's the English of that name.'

18   The knight he rode, the ladye ran,
            A live-long summer's day,
        Till they came to the wan water
            That all men do call Tay.

19   He set his horse head to the water,
            Just thro it for to ride,
        And the ladye was as ready as him
            The waters for to wade.

20   For he had never been as kind-hearted
            As to bid the ladye ride,
        And she had never been so low-hearted
            As for to bid him bide.

21   But deep into the wan water
            There stands a great big stone;
        He turned his wight horse head about,
            Said, Ladye fair, will ye loup on?

She's taken the wand was in her hand   22
   And struck it on the faem,
And before he got the middle-stream
   The ladye was on dry land:
'By help of God and our Lady,
   My help lyes not in your hand!

'I learned it from my mother dear,   23
   Few are there that have learned better,
When I come to deep water,
   I can swim thro like ony otter.

'I learned it from my mother dear,   24
   I find I learnd it for my weel,
When I come to a deep water,
   I can swim thro like ony eel.'

'Turn back, turn back, you ladye fair,   25
   You know not what I see;
There is a ladye in that castle
   That will burn you and me.'
'Betide me weel, betide me wae,
   That ladye I will see.'

She took a ring from her finger,   26
   And gave it the porter for his fee;
Says, Take you that, my good porter,
   And bid the queen speak to me.

And when she came before the queen,   27
   There she fell low down on her knee;
Says, There is a knight into your court
   This day has robbed me.

'O has he robbed you of your gold,   28
   Or has he robbed you of your fee?'
'He has not robbed me of my gold,
   He has not robbed me of my fee;
He has robbed me of my maidenhead,
   The fairest flower of my bodie.'

29   'There is no knight in all my court,
            That thus has robbed thee,
        But you'll have the truth of his right hand,
            Or else for your sake he'll die:

30   'Tho it were Earl Richard, my own brother,
            And, Oh, forbid that it be!'
        Then sighing said the ladye fair,
            I wot the same man is he.

31   The queen called on her merry men,
            Even fifty men and three;
        Earl Richard used to be the first man,
            But now the hindmost man was he.

32   He's taken out one hundred pounds.
            And told it in his glove;
        Says, Take you that, my ladye fair,
            And seek another love.

33   'Oh, no! oh, no!' the ladye cried,
            'That's what shall never be;
        I'll have the truth of your right hand,
            The queen it gave to me.'

34   ['I wish I'd drunken your water, sister,
            When I did drink thus of your ale,
        That for a carl's fair daughter
            It does me gar dree al this bale!]

35   'I wish I had drunk of your water, sister,
            When I did drink your wine,
        That for a carle's fair daughter
            It does gar me dree all this pine!'

36   'May be I am a carle's daughter,
            And may be never nane;
        When ye met me in the greenwood,
            Why did you not let me alane?'

37   'Will you wear the short clothes,
            Or will you wear the side?
        Or will you walk to your wedding,
            Or will you till it ride?'

'I will not wear the short clothes,   38
    But I will wear the side;
I will not walk to my wedding,
    But I to it will ride.'

When he was set upon the horse,   39
    The lady him behin,
Then cauld and eerie were the words
    The twa had them between.

She said, Good e'en, ye nettles tall,   40
    Just there where ye grow at the dyke;
If the auld carline my mother were here,
    Sae weel's she would your pates pyke!

How she would stap you in her poke –   41
    I wot at that she wadna fail –
And boil ye in her auld brass pan,
    And of ye make right good kail!

And she would meal you with millering,   42
    That she gathers at the mill,
And make you thick as ony daigh:
    And when the pan was brimful,

Would mess you up in scuttle-dishes,   43
    Syne bid us sup till we were fou,
Lay down her head upon a poke,
    Then sleep and snore like ony sow.

'Away, away, you bad woman!   44
    For all your vile words grieveth me;
When you hide so little for yourself,
    I'm sure ye'll hide far less for me.

'I wish I had drunk your water, sister,   45
    When that I did drink of your wine,
Since for a carle's fair daughter,
    It aye gars me dree all this pine.'

'May be I am a carle's daughter,   46
    And may be never nane;
When ye met me in the good greenwood,
    Why did you not let me alane?

47   'Gude een, gude een, ye heather-berries,
          As ye're growing on yon hill;
      If the auld carline and her bags were here,
          I wot she would get meat her fill.

48   'Late, late at night, I knit our pokes,
          With even four an twenty knots;
      And in the morn at breakfast time
          I'll carry the keys of an earl's locks.

49   'Late, late at night, I knit our pokes,
          With even four an twenty strings;
      And if you look to my white fingers,
          They have as many gay gold rings.'

50   'Away, away, ye ill woman!
          So sore your vile words grieveth me;
      When you hide so little for yourself,
          I'm sure ye'll hide far less for me.

51   'But if you are a carle's daughter,
          As I take you to be,
      How did you get the gay cloathing,
          In greenwood ye had on thee?'

52   'My mother, she's a poor woman,
          She nursed earl's children three,
      And I got them from a foster-sister,
          For to beguile such sparks as thee.'

53   'But if you be a carle's daughter,
          As I believe you be,
      How did you learn the good Latin
          In greenwood ye spoke to me?'

54   'My mother, she's a mean woman,
          She nursd earl's children three;
      I learnt it from their chaplain,
          To beguile such sparks as ye.'

55   When mass was sung, and bells were rung,
          And all men bound for bed,
      Then Earl Richard and this ladye
          In ae bed they were laid.

He turned his face unto the stock,   56
    And she her's to the stane,
And cauld and dreary was the love
    That was these twa between.

Great mirth was in the kitchen,   57
    Likewise intill the ha,
But in his bed lay Earl Richard,
    Wiping the tears awa.

He wept till he fell fast asleep,   58
    Then slept till light was come;
Then he did hear the gentlemen
    That talked in the room:

Said, Saw ye ever a fitter match,   59
    Betwixt the ane and ither,
The king of Scotland's fair dochter
    And the queen of England's brither?

'And is she the king o Scotland's fair dochter?   60
    This day, O weel is me!
For seven times has my steed been saddled,
    To come to court with thee;
And with this witty lady fair,
    How happy must I be!'

33. Mary Hamilton   [Ch 173M]

Then down cam Queen Marie,   I
    Wi gold links in her hair,
Saying, Marie Mild, where is the child,
    That I heard greet sae sair?

'There was nae child wi me, madam,   2
    There was nae child wi me;
It was but me in a sair cholic,
    When I was like to die.'

3   'I'm not deceived,' Queen Marie said,
    'No, no, indeed not I!
   So Marie Mild, where is the child?
    For sure I heard it cry.'

4   She turned down the blankets fine,
    Likewise the Holland sheet,
   And underneath, there strangled lay
    A lovely baby sweet.

5   'O cruel mother,' said the queen
    'Some fiend possessed thee;
   But I will hang thee for this deed,
    My Marie tho thou be!'

      *   *   *

6   When she cam to the Netherbow Port
    She laught loud laughters three;
   But when she cam to the gallows-foot,
    The saut tear blinded her ee.

7   'Yestreen the Queen had four Maries,
    The night she'll hae but three;
   There was Marie Seton, and Marie Beaton,
    And Marie Carmichael, and me.

8   'Ye mariners, ye mariners,
    That sail upon the sea,
   Let not my father or mother wit
    The death that I maun die!

9   'I was my parents' only hope,
    They neer had ane but me;
   They little thought when I left hame,
    They should nae mair me see!'

34. Archie o Cawfield [*Ch 188D*]

'Seven years have I loved my love,   1
  And seven years my love's loved me,
But now to-morrow is the day
  That billy Archie, my love, must die.'

O then out spoke him Little Dickie,   2
  And still the best fellow was he:
'Had I but five men and my self,
  Then we would borrow billy Archie.'

Out it spoke him Caff o Lin,   3
  And still the worst fellow was he:
'You shall have five men and yourself,
  And I will bear you companye.'

'We will not go like to dragoons,   4
  Nor yet will we like grenadiers,
But we will go like corn-dealers,
  And lay our brechams on our meares.

'And twa of us will watch the road,   5
  And other twa will go between,
And I will go to jail-house door,
  And hold the prisoner unthought lang.'

'Who is this at jail-house door,   6
  So well as they do know the gin?'
'It's I myself,' [said] him Little Dickie,
  'And oh sae fain's I would be in!'

'Away, away, now, Little Dickie!   7
  Away, let all your folly be!
If the Lord Lieutenant come on you,
  Like unto dogs he'll cause you die.'

'Hold you, hold you, billy Archie,   8
  And now let all your folly be!
Tho I die without, you'll not die within,
  For borrowed shall your body be.'

'Away, away, now, Little Dickie!   9
  Away, let all this folly be!
An hundred pounds of Spanish irons
  Is all bound on my fair bodie.'

10   Wi plough-culters and gavellocks
          They made the jail-house door to flee;
      'And in God's name,' said Little Dickie,
          'Cast you the prisoner behind me!'

11   They had not rode a great way off,
          With all the haste that ever could be,
      Till they espied the Lord Lieutenant,
          With a hundred men in's companie.

12   But when they came to wan water,
          It now was rumbling like the sea;
      Then were they got into a strait,
          As great a strait as well could be.

13   Then out did speak him Caff o Lin,
          And aye the warst fellow was he:
      'Now God be with my wife and bairns!
          For fatherless my babes will be.

14   'My horse is young, he cannot swim;
          The water's deep, and will not wade;
      My children must be fatherless,
          My wife a widow, whateer betide.'

15   O then cried out him Little Dickie,
          And still the best fellow was he:
      'Take you my mare, I'll take your horse,
          And Devil drown my mare and thee!'

16   Now they have taken the wan water,
          Tho it was roaring like the sea,
      And whan they got to the other side,
          I wot they bragged right crouselie.

17   'Come thro, come thro now, Lord Lieutenant!
          O do come thro, I pray of thee!
      There is an alehouse not far off,
          We'll dine you and your companye.'

18   'Away, away, now, Little Dickie!
          O now let all your taunting be!
      There's not a man in the king's army
          That would have tried what's done by thee.

'Cast back, cast back my fetters again!   19
　　Cast back my fetters! I say to thee;
And get you gane the way you came,
　　I wish no prisoners like to thee.'

'I have a mare, she's called Meg,   20
　　The best in all our low countrie;
If she gang barefoot till they are done,
　　An ill death may your lordship die!'

35. The Fire of Frendraught [*Ch 196A*]

The eighteenth of October,   1
　　A dismal tale to hear
How good Lord John and Rothiemay
　　Was both burnt in the fire.

When steeds was saddled and well bridled,   2
　　And ready for to ride,
Then out it came her false Frendraught,
　　Inviting them to bide.

Said, 'Stay this night untill we sup,   3
　　The morn untill we dine;
'Twill be a token of good greement
　　'Twixt your good lord and mine.'

'We'll turn again,' said good Lord John;   4
　　'But no,' said Rothiemay,
'My steed's trapand, my bridle's broken,
　　I fear the day I'm fey.'

When mass was sung, and bells was rung,   5
　　And all men bound for bed,
Then good Lord John and Rothiemay
　　In one chamber was laid.

They had not long cast off their cloaths,   6
　　And were but now asleep,
When the weary smoke began to rise,
　　Likewise the scorching heat.

7   'O waken, waken, Rothiemay!
        O waken, brother dear!
    And turn you to our Saviour;
        There is strong treason here.'

8   When they were dressed in their cloaths,
        And ready for to boun,
    The doors and windows was all secur'd,
        The roof-tree burning down.

9   He did him to the wire-window,
        As fast as he could gang;
    Says, Wae to the hands put in the stancheons!
        For out we'll never win.

10   When he stood at the wire-window,
        Most doleful to be seen,
    He did espy her Lady Frendraught,
        Who stood upon the green.

11   Cried, Mercy, mercy, Lady Frendraught!
        Will ye not sink with sin?
    For first your husband killed my father,
        And now you burn his son.

12   O then out spoke her Lady Frendraught,
        And loudly did she cry;
    'It were great pity for good Lord John,
        But none for Rothiemay;
    But the keys are casten in the deep draw-well,
        Ye cannot get away.'

13   While he stood in this dreadful plight,
        Most piteous to be seen,
    There called out his servant Gordon,
        As he had frantic been:

14   'O loup, O loup, my dear master!
        O loup and come to me!
    I'll catch you in my arms two,
        One foot I will not flee.

15   'O loup, O loup, my dear master!
        O loup and come away!
    I'll catch you in my arms two,
        But Rothiemay may lie.'

'The fish shall never swim in the flood,   16
    Nor corn grow through the clay,
Nor the fiercest fire that ever was kindled
    Twin me and Rothiemay.

'But I cannot loup, I cannot come,   17
    I cannot win to thee;
My head's fast in the wire-window,
    My feet burning from me.

'My eyes are seething in my head,   18
    My flesh roasting also,
My bowels are boiling with my blood;
    Is not that a woeful woe?

'Take here the rings from my white fingers,   19
    That are so long and small,
And give them to my lady fair,
    Where she sits in her hall.

'So I cannot loup, I cannot come,   20
    I cannot loup to thee;
My earthly part is all consumed,
    My spirit but speaks to thee.'

Wringing her hands, tearing her hair,   21
    His lady she was seen,
And thus addressed his servant Gordon,
    Where he stood on the green.

'O wae be to you, George Gordon!   22
    An ill death may you die!
So safe and sound as you stand there,
    And my lord bereaved from me.'

'I bad him loup, I bad him come,   23
    I bad him loup to me;
I'd catch him in my arms two,
    A foot I should not flee.   &c.

'He threw me the rings from his white fingers,   24
    Which were so long and small,
To give to you, his lady fair,
    Where you sat in your hall.'   &c.

25   Sophia Hay, Sophia Hay,
            O bonny Sophia was her name,
        Her waiting maid put on her cloaths,
            But I wot she tore them off again.

26   And aft she cried, Ohon! alas! alas!
            A sair heart's ill to win;
        I wan a sair heart when I married him,
            And the day it's well returnd again.

[Ch 198A] 36. Bonny John Seton

1   Upon the eighteenth day of June,
            A dreary day to see,
        The southern lords did pitch their camp
            Just at the bridge of Dee.

2   Bonny John Seton of Pitmeddin,
            A bold baron was he,
        He made his testament ere he went out,
            The wiser man was he.

3   He left his land to his young son,
            His lady her dowry,
        A thousand crowns to his daughter Jean,
            Yet on the nurse's knee.

4   Then out came his lady fair,
            A tear into her ee;
        Says, Stay at home, my own good lord,
            O stay at home with me!

5   He looked over his left shoulder,
            Cried, Souldiers, follow me!
        O then she looked in his face,
            An angry woman was she:
        'God send me back my steed again,
            But neer let me see thee!'

His name was Major Middleton   6
    That manned the bridge of Dee,
His name was Colonel Henderson
    That let the cannons flee.

His name was Major Middleton   7
    That manned the bridge of Dee,
And his name was Colonel Henderson
    That dung Pitmeddin in three.

Some rode on the black and grey,   8
    And some rode on the brown,
But the bonny John Seton
    Lay gasping on the ground.

Then bye there comes a false Forbes,   9
    Was riding from Driminere;
Says, Here there lies a proud Seton;
    This day they ride the rear.

Cragievar said to his men,   10
    'You may play on your shield;
For the proudest Seton in all the lan
    This day lies on the field.'

'O spoil him! spoil him!' cried Cragievar,   11
    'Him spoiled let me see;
For on my word,' said Cragievar,
    'He had no good will at me.'

They took from him his armour clear,   12
    His sword, likewise his shield;
Yea, they have left him naked there,
    Upon the open field.

The Highland men, they're clever men   13
    At handling sword and shield,
But yet they are too naked men
    To stay in battle field.

The Highland men are clever men   14
    At handling sword or gun,
But yet they are too naked men
    To bear the cannon's rung.

15 For a cannon's roar in a summer night
     Is like thunder in the air;
   There's not a man in Highland dress
     Can face the cannon's fire.

37. Eppie Morrie

1 Four-and-twenty Highland men
     Came a' from Carrie side
   To steal awa Eppie Morrie,
     Cause she would not be a bride.

2 Out it's came her mother,
     It was a moonlight night,
   She could not see her daughter,
     Their swords they shin'd so bright.

3 'Haud far awa frae me, mother,
     Haud far awa frae me;
   There's not a man in a' Strathdon
     Shall wedded be with me.'

4 They have taken Eppie Morrie,
     And horse back bound her on,
   And then awa to the minister,
     As fast as horse could gang.

5 He's taken out a pistol,
     And set it to the minister's breast:
   'Marry me, marry me, minister,
     Or else I'll be your priest.'

6 'Haud far awa frae me, good sir,
     Haud far awa frae me;
   For there's not a man in all Strathdon
     That shall married be with me.'

7 'Haud far awa frae me, Willie,
     Haud far awa frae me;
   For I darna avow to marry you,
     Except she's as willing as ye.'

They have taken Eppie Morrie,⁣   8
  Since better could nae be,
And they're awa to Carrie side,
  As fast as horse could flee.

When mass was sung, and bells were rung,   9
  And all were bound for bed,
Then Willie an Eppie Morrie
  In one bed they were laid.

'Haud far awa frae me, Willie,   10
  Haud far awa frae me;
Before I'll lose my maidenhead
  I'll try my strength with thee.'

She took the cap from off her head   11
  And threw it to the way;
Said, Ere I lose my maidenhead,
  I'll fight with you till day.

Then early in the morning,   12
  Before her clothes were on,
In came the maiden of Scalletter,
  Gown and shirt alone.

'Ge up, get up, young woman,   13
  And drink the wine wi me;'
'You might have called me maiden,
  I'm sure as leal as thee.'

'Wally fa you, Willie,   14
  That ye could nae prove a man
And taen the lassie's maidenhead!
  She would have hired your han.'

'Haud far awa frae me, lady,   15
  Haud far awa frae me;
There's not a man in a' Strathdon
  The day shall wed wi me.'

Soon in there came Belbordlane,   16
  With a pistol on every side:
'Come awa hame, Eppie Morrie,
  And there you'll be my bride.'

17 'Go get to me a horse, Willie,
    And get it like a man,
   And send me back to my mother
    A maiden as I cam.

18 'The sun shines oer the westlin hills;
    By the light lamp of the moon,
   Just saddle your horse, young John Forsyth,
    And whistle, and I'll come soon.'

[Ch 231D] 38. The Earl of Errol

1 O Errol's place is a bonny place,
    It stands upon yon plain;
   The flowers on it grow red and white,
    The apples red and green.
     The ranting o't and the danting o't,
      According as ye ken,
     The thing they ca the danting o't,
      Lady Errol lies her lane.

2 O Errol's place is a bonny place,
    It stands upon yon plain;
   But what's the use of Errol's place?
    He's no like other men.

3 'As I cam in by yon canal,
    And by yon bowling-green,
   I might hae pleased the best Carnegy
    That ever bore that name.

4 'As sure's your name is Kate Carnegy,
    And mine is Gibbie Hay,
   I'll gar your father sell his land,
    Your tocher for to pay.'

5 'To gar my father sell his land,
    Would it not be a sin,
   To give it to a naughtless lord
    That couldna get a son?'

Now she is on to Edinburgh,   6
   For to try the law,
And Errol he has followed her,
   His manhood for to shaw.

Then out it spake her sister,   7
   Whose name was Lady Jane;
'Had I been Lady Errol,' she says,
   'Or come of sic a clan,
I would not in this public way
   Have sham'd my own gudeman.'

But Errol got it in his will   8
   To choice a maid himsel,
And he has taen a country-girl,
   Came in her milk to sell.

He took her by the milk-white hand,   9
   And led her up the green,
And twenty times he kissd her there,
   Before his lady's een.

He took her by the milk-white hand,   10
   And led her up the stair;
Says, Thrice three hundred pounds I'll gie
   To you to bear an heir.

He kept her there into a room   11
   Three quarters of a year,
And when the three quarters were out
   A braw young son she bear.

'Tak hame your daughter, Carnegy,   12
   And put her till a man,
For Errol he cannot please her,
   Nor any of his men.'

[Ch 302]   39. Young Bearwell

1   When two lovers love each other well,
       Great sin it were them to twinn;
    And this I speak from Young Bearwell;
       He loved a lady young,
    The Mayor's daughter of Birktoun-brae,
       That lovely, leesome thing.

2   One day when she was looking out,
       When washing her milk-white hands,
    That she beheld him Young Bearwell,
       As he came in the sands.

3   Says, Wae's me for you, Young Bearwell,
       Such tales of you are tauld;
    They'll cause you sail the salt sea so far
       As beyond Yorkisfauld.

4   .   .   .   .
       .   .   .   .
    'O shall I bide in good greenwood,
       Or stay in bower with thee?'

5   'The leaves are thick in good greenwood,
       Would hold you from the rain;
    And if you stay in bower with me
       You will be taken and slain.

6   'But I caused build a ship for you
       Upon Saint Innocent's day;
    I'll bid Saint Innocent be your guide,
       And Our Lady, that meikle may.
    You are a lady's first true-love,
       God carry you well away!'

7   Then he sailed east, and he sailed west,
       By many a comely strand;
    At length a puff of northern wind
       Did blow him to the land.

8   When he did see the king and court,
       Were playing at the ba;
    Gave him a harp into his hand,
       Says, Stay, Bearwell, and play.

He had not been in the king's court   9
   A twelvemonth and a day,
Till there came lairds and lords anew
   To court that lady gay.

They wooed her with brooch and ring,   10
   They nothing could keep back;
The very charters of their lands
   Into her hands they pat.

She's done her down to Heyvalin,   11
   With the light of the moon;
Says, Will ye do this deed for me,
   And will ye do it soon?

'Will ye go seek him Young Bearwell,   12
   On seas wherever he be?
And if I live and bruik my life
   Rewarded ye shall be.'

'Alas, I am too young a skipper,   13
   So far to sail the faem;
But if I live and bruik my life
   I'll strive to bring him hame.'

So he has saild east and then saild west,   14
   By many a comely strand,
Till there came a blast of northern wind
   And blew him to the land.

And there the king and all his court   15
   Were playing at the ba;
Gave him a harp into his hand,
   Says, Stay, Heyvalin, and play.

He has tane up the harp in hand,   16
   And unto play went he,
And Young Bearwell was the first man
   In all that companie.

      *   *   *

40. The Young Laird of Craigstoun

1   Father, she said, you have done me wrong
     For ye have married me on a child young man
     For ye have married me on a child young man,
     And my bonny love is long a growing.

2   Daughter, said he, I have done you no wrong
     For I have married you on a heritor of land
     He's likewise possess'd of many bill and band
     And He'll be daily growing.
     Growing, deary, growing, growing
     Growing, said the bonny maid,
     Slowly's my bonny love growing.

3   Daughter said he, if ye do weel
     Ye will put your husband away to the scheel,
     That he of learning may gather great skill,
     And he'll be daily growing.
     Growing &c.

4   Now young Craigston to the College is gane
     And left his Lady making great mane
     That he's so long a growing
     growing &c.

5   She dress'd herself in robes of green
     They were right comely to be seen
     She was the picture of Venus the Queen
     And she's to the College to see him.
     Growing &c.

6   Then all the collesiners was playing at the ba'
     But young Craigstone was the flower of them a'
     He said – play on, my school fellows a'
     For I see my sister coming.

7   Now down into the College park
     They walked about till it was dark,
     Then he lifted up her fine holland sark –
     And she had no reason to complain of his growing
     growing &c.

In his twelfth year he was a married man,   8
In his thirteenth year there he got a son,
And in his fourteenth year his grave grew green,
And that was an end of his growing –
growing, deary &c.

The Modern
Tradition (i): The Ballads
of Bell Robertson

41. The Elfin Knight

1   There stands three trumpeters on yon hill,
          Blaw, blaw, blaw, winds blaw;
      Blaws their trumpet baith loud an' shrill,
          An' the wind blaws aye my plaid awa.

2   'Gin I'd his trumpet in my kist,
      An' were in the lad's arms that I like best.'

3   'What wad ye dee in a young man's arms,
      An' you yoursel' in such young charms?'

4   'My sister Jean's younger than I,
      She was wedded yesterday.'

5   'Gin ye wad be wed wi me,
      There's ae thing ye maun to me dee.

6   'I maun hae a fine linen sark,
      Without a stitch o needlewark.

7   'Ye maun wash't in yon draw-well,
      Where water never sprang nor fell.

8   'Ye maun dry't on yon hawthorn,
      That hasna been in blossom sin man was born.'

9   'Gin I mak a sark to thee,
      There's something ye maun dee for me.

10   'My father has an acre o lan',
      An' ye maun ploo it wi your han'.

11   'Ye maun sow it wantin corn,
      An' roll it all wi a sheep's shank-bone.

12   'Ye maun shear't wi a scythe o leather,
      An' bind it all wi peacock's feather.

13   'Ye maun stook it in the sea,
      An' bring the wheat sheaf dry to me.

14   'Ye maun winnow on your loof,
      An' stack it all in your right hand glove.

15   'An gin ye work noo all this wark,
      Come to me an' ye'se get your sark.'

16   'Since ye've answered the questions so fine,
      Come what will an' ye sall be mine.'

42. Lady Isabel and the Elf-Knight

O heard ye o a bloody knight 1
   Lives in the west countrie?
He has betrayed eight ladies fair
   An' he's drooned them in the sea.

He has come to May Colvin, 2
   She was her father's heir,
She was the beauty o them a',
   I solemnly declare.

He said: 'I am a Baron Knight 3
   Has lands thirty an' three,
An' ye'se be lady o them a',
   Fair May, an ye'll go wi me.'

'O haud your tongue, noo, good Sir John, 4
   I pray let me alane,
For unless I get my parents' consent,
   It's wi you I daurna gang.'

'Your parents' leave ye soon shall have, 5
   To this they will agree;
For I have sworn a solemn oath,
   Fair May, that ye'se go wi me.'

Oot o his arm he pulled a charm, 6
   An' he stuck it in her sleeve,
An' he's made her to go wi him
   Without her parents' leave.

Five hundred pounds o good red gold 7
   She took wi her along;
The swiftest steed her father had
   She took to ride upon.

So privately they went away 8
   There was none to hear or see,
Till they cam to yon fatal end
   That they call beenie an' by.

9   The fatal rocks were tall an' steep,
          There was none to hear her cry.
      'Light doon, light doon noo, May Colvin,
          Light doon an' speak to me,
      For here I drooned eight ladies fair,
          An' the ninth ane ye maun be.'

10   'Is this your bowers an lofty towers
          So costly, rich, an' gay?
      Or is it for my gold,' she said,
          'Ye're to tak my life away?'

11   'Cast aff,' he said, 'your gown o silk
          So costly, rich, an' grand,
      It is too costly an' too fine
          To rot on the sea sand.

12   Cast aff,' he said, 'your Holland smock,
          It's bordered wi the lawn,
      It is too costly an' too fine
          To rot on the sea stran'.'

13   Her jewels fine she then put aff,
          An' thus she made her moan:
      'Hae mercy on a virgin young,
          I pray you, good Sir John.
      Lat it never be said ye killed a maid
          Before her wedding come.

14   'But turn ye roon noo, good Sir John,
          About your back to me,
      For it is not comely for a man
          A naked woman to see.'

15   Then as Sir John he turned him roon.
          She's thrown him in the sea,
      Said, 'Lie ye there, ye traitor false,
          For ye thought to slay me.
      Although ye stripped me to the skin,
          Ye'se get your clothes fae me.'

16   Her jewels fine she then put on,
          So costly, rich, an' brave,
      Her steed on then she mounts hersel,
          So weel as she did behave.

Fan she was on o her milk-white steed,   17
   He was both swift an' free,
She lighted at her father's yetts
   Before the clock struck three.

She called for the stable-groom,   18
   He was her waiting-man,
As soon's he heard that lady's voice,
   He cam wi hat in han'.

Then oot it spak the pretty parrot,   19
   An' she said, 'Fair May Colvin,
O what did ye wi good Sir John,
   That gaed oot wi you yestreen.'

'O hold your tongue, ye pretty parrot;   20
   An ye talk no more to me,
Your cage it is o timmer fine,
   But o red gowd it sall be.'

Then first she tauld her mother dear   21
   O' the deed that she had done,
An' then she tauld her father dear
   Concerning false Sir John.

So privately as they went away   22
   By the dawning o the day,
Till they came to yon fatal end
   That ye call beenie an' by.

Up hae they taen him, false Sir John,   23
   To yonder pleasant green,
An' there they buried false Sir John,
   For fear he had been seen.

43. Leesome Brand   [*Ch 15*]

'The morn is the day,' she said,   1
   'I in my father's court maun stan',
An' I'll be set in a chair o gold,
   To see gin I be maid or nane.

2   'Ye go into my father's stable,
        The steeds stan' there both wight an' able.

3   'Ye gie ony o them upon the breast,
        The swiftest will gie his head a cast.

4   'Ye tak him oot upon the green,
        An' tak me shortly on ahin.'

5   He went into her father's stable,
        The steeds stood there both wight an' able.

6   He gae ane o them upon the breast,
        The swiftest gae his head a cast.

7   He took him oot upon the green,
        An' took her shortly on ahin.

8   But they hadna ridden a mile but twa,
        Till aff o the horse she was like to fa'.

9   They hadna ridden a mile but three,
        Till on the horse she was like to dee.

10   'O, gin I lout me to my tae,
        My very back will go in twa;

11   'An gin I lout me to my knee,
        My silver sneeds they'll go in three.

12   'Ye tak your flint an' fleerishin,
        An' kindle up a fire richt seen.

13   'Ye dee ye doon to yon greenwood,
        An' shortsome you wi deer an' rae.

14   'See that ye harm not yon ae fite hin',
        For she is come o women kin'.'

15   He's taen his flint an' fleerishin,
        An' kindled up a fire richt seen.

16   He's done him down to yon greenwood,
        To shortsome him wi deer an' rae.

17   He took such delight in deer an' rae,
        That he his lady clean forgot.

Till by it cam yon ae white hin',   18
That min't him on his lady syne.

Then he has to his lady gane,   19
An' aye as fast as gang could he;

An' there he found his lady dead,   20
An' his little young son laid at her head.

His mother lay o'er castle wa',   21
    An' she beheld both dale an' down,
An' she beheld Sir Lishen Brand,
    He was comin rakin to the town.

'Ye get me pipers to play,' she says,   22
    'An ladies to dance in a reel,
For here is my son Lishen Brand,
    An' he's comin rakin to the town.'

'Ye get nae pipers to play, mother,   23
    Nor ladies to dance in a reel,
For I am your son Lishen Brand,
    But I'm comin sorry to the town.

'For I hae lost my gay gold knife,   24
I loved it dearer than my life;

'An' I have lost a better thing,   25
I hae lost the sheath that the knife lay in.'

'Is there not a smith in a' my lan'   26
Could mak to you a knife again?

'Is there souter in a' my lan'   27
Could seam to you a sheath again?'

'There's nae a smith in a' your lan'   28
Could shape the blade oot o the tang;

'There's nae a souter in a' your lan'   29
Could sew to me a sheath again.'

'O ye hae lost your lady gay   30
An' ye hae lost your little young son.

31   'But do ye to your mother's bed-head,
            Ye'll find a horn has hung lang,
        An' there ye'll find three draps o bleed
            That has hung there since one was born.

32   'Ye drap twa on your lady gay,
            An' ane upon your little young son,
        An' ye'll fin' them as life-livin
            As the first hour that ye got them in.'

33   He's done him to his mother's bed-head,
            An' found a horn had hung lang,
        An' there he found three draps o bleed
            That had hung there since one was born.

34   He drappit twa on his lady gay,
            An' ane upon his little young son,
        An' he fan them as life-livin
            As the first hour that he got them in.

44. Hind Horn

1   Hind Horn frank an' Hind Horn free,
        Whaur was ye born, in what kintrie?

2   'O I was born in the forest sae free,
        An' a' my forbears before me.

3   'Seven years I sair'd the King,
        Fae him I wat I gat naething,

4   'But one sight o his daughter Jane,
        An' that was thro' a gay gold ring.'

5   Lang did he dwell aneath the grun',
        At length to the lady's chamber he cam;

6   Said, 'I am gaun to sail the sea,
        Some love token ye'se gie to me.'

7   'O I'll gie you a gay gold ring,
        But than a birdie sweet singin;

'As lang's your ring does keep its hue,   8
Remember aye your love is true.

'As soon as your love loves a man,   9
Your birdie will tak flight, an' it will flee hame.'

Seven years he sail'd the sea,   10
Before he lookit his ring intee;

An' when he lookit his ring upon,   11
The gay gold ring it was pale an' wan.

An' when he opened his silver wain,   12
His birdie had taen flight an' had flown hame.

He hoised up sails an' cam to lan',   13
An' there he met an aul beggar man.

'What news, what news, ye silly aul man,   14
What news, what news, hae ye to me?'

'Nae news, nae news,' the aul man said,   15
'But the morn's our young Queen's weddin day.'

'Ye'll gie me your beggin weed,   16
An' I'll gie you my robes o reid.'

'Your robes o reid's ower high for me,   17
My beggin weed's ower low for thee.' –

But pairt o richt an' pairt by wrang,   18
The beggin weed fae the beggar he wan.

'When ye gae up to the King's gate,   19
Ower a strae ye canna step.

'Ye'll seek meat fae Peter and ye'll seek meat fae Paul,   20
An' meat fae the high to the low o them all;

'But ye do tak no meat fae none,   21
Till it come fae the bride's ain han'.'

The porter's done him up the stair,   22
An' he bowed low doon on his knee. –
'Win up, win up, my proud porter,
An' aye what maks ye bow to me?'

23   'O I've been porter at this gate
          This thirty years noo an' three,
      But sic a beggar's at them the day,
          The like o him did I never see.

24   'He seeks meat fae Peter an' meat fae Paul,
      An' meat fae the high to the low o them all,

25   'But he will tak no meat fae none
      Till it comes fae the bride's ain han'.'

26   The bride cam trippin doon the stair,
      Wi the kames o' reid gowd in her hair,

27   A glass o reid wine in her han',
      An' a' was for the silly aul man.

28   He took the wine an' he drank it a',
      An' into the cup the ring did fa'.

29   An' when she lookit the ring upon,
      An' aye an' sae weel as she did it ken.

30   'O whaur got ye that ring?' said she;
      'Got ye it sailin on the sea?

31   'Got ye't by sea, or got ye't by lan'?
      Or got ye it on a droon't man's han'?'

32   'I got na't by sea, nor got I't by lan',
      Nor got I't on a droon't man's han',

33   'But I got it in my wooin gay,
      An' I'll gie't you on your weddin day.'

34   She tore the reid gowd fae her heid,
      Says, 'I'll gang wi you, love, an' beg my breid.'

35   She tore the reid gowd fae her hair,
      Says, 'I'll gang wi you, love, for ever mair.'

36   He loot the clootit cloak doon fa',
      An' he stood reid gowd brisk an' braw.

37   An' pairt by richt an' pairt by wrang,
      The bride fae the silly bridegroom he wan.

45. Bonnie Annie [Ch 24]

'. . . my honey,   1
What more can a woman do than I'll do for you?'

'O captain, tak gold, O captain, tak money,   2
An' sail to dry lan' for the sake o my honey.'

'How can I tak gold, how can I tak money?   3
There's fey folk on my ship, she winna sail for me.'

'Ye tak me by the fingers, ye lift me up gently,   4
An' throw me o'erboard, an' hae nae pity on me.'

He's taen her by the fingers, an' did lift her up heely,   5
An' thrown her o'erboard: she was his ain dearie.

Her goon it was wide, an' her petticoat narrow,   6
An' she swam afore them till they cam to Yarrow.

An' ca'in to dry lan', his love was afore them,   7
An' lyin on the stran' . . .

The baby was born an' lyin at her feet;   8
For the loss o his bonnie love sore did he weep.

He's caused mak a kist o the gowd sae yellow,   9
An' they a' three sleep in the braes o Yarrow.

46. Kempy Kay [Ch 33]

Wash, wash, ye foul heap,   1
   Wash an' mak ye clean;
There's wooers comin to the toon,
   An' yer foul face maun be seen.
      An' bar weel the bower door, O, weel O,
      An' bar aye the bower door weel.

She got a little wee sup water   2
   Standin in a dish, ay, ay,
An' aye as she scrapit
   Her ugly face to wash, ay, ay.

3   Ilka hair upon her heid
            Was like a heather cowe,
       An' ilka loose below that
            Was like a lintseed bow.

4   Ilka pap upon her breast
            Was like a saffron bag, ay, ay,
       An' her twa han's at her back,
            Was rivin aff the scab, ay, ay.

                    *   *   *

5   Fan he cam hame fae his huntin,
            An' that was her desire,
       Afore his heels wan fae the door
            His nose was at the fire.

6   She gae him a napkin,
            It she'd keepit lang, ay, ay,
       An' he gae her a guid gowd ring
            Made oot o the auld brass pan, ay, ay.

[Ch 44]   47. The Twa Magicians

1   She became a ship, a ship,
                An' sailed upon the sea;
            An' he became a mariner,
                Aboard o her gaed he.

2   Sayin, Bide, lassie, bide,
                An' aye he bade her bide,
            An' be the brookie smith's wife,
                An' that'll lay your pride.

48. Captain Wedderburn's [*Ch 46*] Courtship

The Laird o' Russel's daughter   1
  In the wood walking her lane,
And by came Captain Wedderburn
  A servant to the King.

He said unto his livery man,   2
  Wer't not against the law,
I would tak' her to my ain bed,
  And lay her neist the wa'.

I'm in my father's wood she said   3
  Among my father's trees
And ye may lat me walk awhile
  My young man if ye please.

For the supper bells they will be rung,   4
  And I'll be missed awa',
And my father winna eat a bit
  Gin I be missed awa'.

It's O my bonnie lady,   5
  I will tell you my name,
My name is Captain Wedderburn
  A servant to the King.

Though your father an' a' his men were here,   6
  I wad say to them a',
That we'se baith lie in ae bed,
  And ye'se lie neist the wa'.

Oh haud awa young man, she said,   7
  And dinna trouble me,
For I winna gang to your bed
  Till ye grant me askin's three.

And answer me as I ask at thee,   8
  And that's by ane and twa
Afore I gang to your bed
  To lie at stock or wa'.

9   Oh I maun hae to my supper
          A chicken without a bone,
       And I maun hae to my supper
          A cherry without a stone.

10   And I maun hae to my supper
          A bird without a gaw
       Before I come to your bed
          To lie at stock or wa'.

11   A chicken when it's in the egg,
          In it there is no bone,
       A cherry when it's in the bloom
          In it there is no stone.

12   The dove she is a gentle bird
          She flies without a gaw;
       And we'se baith lie in ae bed,
          And ye'se lie neist the wa'.

13   O haud awa' young man, she said,
          And dinna me perplex,
       For I winna gang to your bed
          Till ye answer questions six

14   And answer me as I ask at thee,
          And that's by twa and twa,
       Afore I gang to your bed
          To lie at stock or wa'.

15   Oh what is greener than the grass?
          What's higher than the trees?
       And what is waur than woman's wish?
          What deeper than the seas?

16   What bird sings first? What wood buds next?
          And what time does it fa'?
       Before I gang to your bed
          To lie at stock or wa'.

17   Oh holly's greener than the grass;
          Heaven's higher than the trees;
       The devil's waur than woman's wish;
          Hell's deeper than the seas.

The cock crows first; southronwood buds next;   18
   In December it does fa';
And we'se baith lie in ae bed,
   And ye'se lie neist the wa'.

Oh haud awa young man, she said,   19
   And dinna come me near,
For I winna come to your bed
   Till ye grant me askin's four.

And answer me as I ask at thee,   20
   And that's by twa and twa,
Before I gang to your bed
   To lie at stock or wa'.

Oh I maun hae a silk mantle   21
   That waft gaed never through,
And I maun hae a cherry
   That in December grew.

A sparrow's horn, a priest unborn,   22
   For to join us twa,
Before I gang to your bed
   To lie at stock or wa'.

My mither has a silk mantle   23
   That waft gaed never through
There is a tree in my father's yard
   For winter cherries grows.

A sparrow's horn's easy got   24
   There's ane on ilka claw,
And ane upon the gab o' it,
   And ye sall get them a'.

A priest is standing at the door   25
   Just ready to come in,
No man can say that he was born
   No man without sin.

A hole was cut in's mother's side,   26
   And out there he did fa', –
And we'se baith lie in ae bed,
   And ye'se lie neist the wa'.

27   Oh little did the lady ken
            In the mornin' fan she rase,
        That that day was to be the last
            O' a' her single days.

28   She wedded Captain Wedderburn,
            A man she never saw,
        And they both lie in ae bed,
            And she lies neist the wa'.

29   And among all the King's whole realms
            There's not a blither twa,
        For they both lie in ae bed,
            And she lies neist the wa'.

[Ch 47]   49. Proud Lady Margaret

1   'What is your will with me, young man,
            What is your will with me?' –
        'My will with you, fair maid, he said,
            'Is your lover till I dee.'

2   'Your lover till ye dee,' she said,
            'Your lover till ye dee?
        I've slichted mony a better man,
            That in their grave lies green.

3   'My father was laird o seven castles,
            My mither was lady o three,
        An' a' their gowd an' a' their gear,
            There's nane to heir't but me.'

4   'Gin your father was laird o seven castles,
            An' your mither was lady o three,
        I am William thy brother
            That died beyond the sea,
        An' I canna get rest into my grave
            For the daily pride o thee.'

            *   *   *

'Is there nae room at your heid, brother?   5
    Is there nae room at your feet?
Is there nae room at your side, brother,
    For a lady like me to sleep?'

'There's nae room at my heid, sister,   6
    There's nae room at my feet,
There's nae room at my side, sister,
    For a lady like you to sleep;
For when I lie down into my grave,
    The worms around me creep.'

50. Sir Patrick Spens   [*Ch 58*]

The king he sits in Dunfermline   1
    A-drinkin at the wine,
An' he called for the best skipper
    In Fife or yet London.

Oot it spak an aul seaman,   2
    Steed by the king's ain knee,
Says, 'Patrick Spens is the best skipper
    That ever sailed the sea.'

The king he's written a broad letter,   3
    An' sealed it wi's ain han',
An' sent it to young Patrick Spens,
    Lay far ayont the faem.

'To Norowa, to Norowa,   4
    To Norowa owre the faem,
The king's daughter to Norowa,
    'Tis thou maun hae her hame.'

Whan he leukit the letter on,   5
    An' a licht lauch gae he,
But afore he read the letter ower,
    The tears blinded his e'e.

6   'O wha is this,' said Patrick Spens,
                     'That's taul the king o me?
                Altho it were my ae brither,
                     Some ill-death may he dee.'

[Then he speaks of the dangers of going to Norway at that season; but he did go, and was to stay till the weather was better; but the courtiers were jealous and said he was staying –]

7   Wastin the king's monie,
                     Likewise the queenie's fee.

8   'How can it be?' said Patrick Spens,
                     'I pray, how can it be?
                I've a bow o gowd upon my ship,
                     An' anither o white monie.

9   'Eat an' drink, my merry men all,
                     An' see 'at ye be weel forn,
                For come it weet or come it win',
                     Our good ship sails the morn.'

[They sailed, the storm rose, and they fought as well as they could, but in vain – they were all lost –]

10   An' four-an-twenty gay ladies
                     Wi their bibles in their han',
                They steed waitin Patrick Spens,
                     Come sailin to dry lan'.

11   But lang, lang, will this ladies wyte,
                     An' langer will they stan',
                Afore they see young Patrick Spens
                     Come sailin to dry lan'.

51. Robin Hood and Allen a Dale

One day, as bauld Robin sat in the wood,   1
   Below a greenwood tree,
And there he spied a handsome young man
   Going tripping along the highway O,
   Going tripping along the highway O.

Next day as bauld Robin sat in the wood,   2
   Below that same green tree,
And there he spied that same young man
   Coming drooping along the highway O.

Little John he bent his bow,   3
   And set an arrow therein,
To draw him on to his master,
   His malison for to win O.

'What is your will,' the young man said,   4
   'What is your will wi me?' –
'Have you any money,' said bauld Robin,
   'For my merry young men and me O?'

'I have nothing,' the young man said,   5
   'But five shillings and a ring
That I hae keepit this lang seven year
   To gie at my wedding O.

'Yesterday I should have married a may,   6
   But awa fae me she's taen:
She's chosen to be an old knight's delight,
   For which my poor heart it is slain O.'

'What is your name?' said bauld Robin,   7
   'I pray you to me tell.' –
'That I will,' the young man said,
   'For they call me young Allen-a-dale O.'

'How many miles is't to your true love?   8
   I pray you to me tell.' –
'That I will,' the young man said,
   'For they tell me it's scarce five mile O.'

9   'What would you give,' said bauld Robin,
            'O' ready gold or fee
        To bear you on to your true love,
            And deliver her safe to thee O?'

10   'I hae nothing,' the young man said,
            'O ready gold or fee,
        But I will swear a solemn oath
            That your true servant I'll be O.'

11   He's taen his harp into his hand,
            Gaed harping ower the plain.
        Till he came to the bishop's gates,
            Where young Allen would a-married been O.

12   'If ye be a harper,' the bishop said,
            'Ye're dear welcome to me' –
        'Ye'se hae nane o my harping,' said bauld Robin,
            'Till the bride and the bridegroom I see O.'

13   Out there came an aged knight,
            He was both infirm and old;
        He had a lady at his back
            Shone like the glittering gold O.

14   'Tis an unmeet marriage,' bauld Robin said,
            'I see that you hae here;
        But now when we're all in the very churchyard,
            The bride she must choose her own dear O.'

15   'For no, for no,' the bishop said,
            'For that must not be done;
        For they must be three times proclaimed in the church,
            By the laws of our sovereign O.'

16   He put his horn to his mouth,
            And blew baith loud and shrill,
        And threescore and ten o bauld Robin's men
            Came tripping in over the hill O.

17   Aff hae they taen the bishop's coat,
            And they put it on Little John:
        'And be my seeth,' said bauld Robin Hood,
            'It's the mounting that maketh the man O.'

Little John did mount the choir,   18
   And oh as the people leuch
To hear them 7 times proclaimed in the church,
   As if 3 times had not been eneuch.

'Who gives the bride to the bridegroom?'   19
   Said bauld Robin, 'It's I;
And he that taks her fae young Allen,
   Sae dear as he sall her buy O.'

And now, to end my merry song,   20
   The bride shines like a queen,
And she's awa to good greenwood
   Amo the leaves sae green O.

52. The Death of   [*Ch 170*]
Queen Jane

'O women, O women, O women,' cried she,   1
'You'll send for my mother, she'll come and see me.'

They sent for her mother, who instantly came: 2
'What ails you, my daughter, you look pale and wan?'

'O mother, O mother, O mother,' cried she,   3
'You'll send for King Henry, he'll come and see me.'

They sent for King Henry, who instantly came: 4
'What ails you, my lady, you look pale and wan?'

'King Henry, King Henry, King Henry,' cried she,   5
'You'll send for a doctor to come and see me.'

He sent for a doctor, who instantly came: 6
'What ails you, my Queen, you look pale and wan?'

'O doctor, O doctor, O doctor,' cried she,   7
'You'll open my left side, and see what ails me.'

She wept and she wailed, she fell into a swoon,   8
Till they opened her left side, and a young prince was found.

9   She wept and she wailed, she wrung her hands sore,
       But the pride of Old England will flourish no more.

10   Black was the kitchen, and black was the hall,
       And black was the aprons that hung on them all.

11   And black were the women attending Queen Jane,
       But bonnie King Henry lay weeping him lane.

[*Ch 178; Last Leaves B*] 53. Edom o Gordon

1   'Faur will I get a winter house
           For my merry men an me?' –
       'Ye'll dee ye on to bonnie Corgraff,
           For there's neen but ae ladye.'

                    *   *   *

2   'Come here, come here, noo, Captain Carr,
           Tak oot the querren stane;
       Come here, come here noo, Captain Carr,
           An' fire to her lat in.'

3   'O woe be to that Captain Carr,
           Some ill death may he dee,
       For seven year he was my man,
           An' I paid him well his fee;
       I paid him ilka plack an' pun,
           The table o Cragie wi.'

4   'O seven year I was your man,
           An' ye paid me weel my fee,
       But noo I am Tam Gordon's man,
           I maun either do or dee.'

                    *   *   *

5   Oot it spak her youngest son,
           For on the green gaed he:
       'O wae's me for the bonnie neerice
           That goes wi bairn to me;
       I'll kep ye in my bonnie cloak lap,
           An' a foot I winna flee.'

She's taen a towel in ilka han,   6
    An' she lap the castle wa';
He was as true, an' she never did rue,
    For he didna lat her fa'.

Then oot it spak her daughter Jane,   7
    For in her bower sat she:
'Gin I'd a towel in ilka han,
    I wad loup the castle wa';
The Gordons they do gang sae thick,
    They wadna lat me fa'.'

'For no, for no, my daughter Jane,   8
    For no, that maunna be,
For ye maun stay within this bower,
    An' dee this death wi me.'

Then oot it spak her eldest son,   9
    On the castle head stood he:
'Gie ower your house, mother,' he said,
    'Or the fire will gar us dee.

'I shot wi your guns, mother,   10
    Till I can nae langer stan';
I shot wi your guns, mother,
    Till I'm a' brunt, fit an' han'.'

54. Edom o Gordon [*Ch 178; Last Leaves C*]

[Tam Edison was told to let in the fire. The lady said: –]
                'Gin I dee within this bower,   1
                    I winna dee my leen;
                There is three on ilka side o me,
                    An' ane my sides atween.'

                Then oot it spak her ain good lord,   2
                    For on the sea sailed he:
                'O bonnie Corgraff is a' on fire,
                    Good preserve my lady gay.

3   'I wad gie a' my bonnie lans,
     I wad gie them ane an' a',
  That on the taps o bonnie Corgraff
     There wad ae cauld blast blaw.

4   'I wad gie a' my bonnie lan's,
     Faur they lie oot an' in,
  That on the taps o bonnie Corgraff
     There wad blaw ae blast o win'.'

[Then he sailed to land, got a horse, and rode home.]

5   He lap into the big, big fire,
     Baith boots an' spurs an' a',
  An' he's taen a kiss o's own true love,
     An' her body fell in twa.

6   'O I hae corn, an' I hae bere,
     An' barley in a bing,
  But I wad gie it a' this nicht
     To hear my lady sing.'

[Ch 219]   55. The Gardener

1   There lived a lass now near han' by,
     Who many sweethearts had,
  An' the gardener laddie viewed them a',
     Jist as they cam an' gaed;
  An' the gardener laddie viewed them a',
     Jist as they cam an' gaed.

2   The gardener laddie viewed them a',
     An' he said he hadna skeel,
  'But an I wad gae as aft's the rest,
     They wad say I were a feel.

3   'I'm sure she's nae a proper lass,
     Neither handsome, tight, nor tall';
  But another young man that stood by
     Said, 'Slight her not at all.

'For we are a' come o womankin',
  If we wad cal to min',
An' it's unto women for their sake
  We surely sud be kin'.'   4

'Well, if I thought her worth my pains,
  Unto her I wad go,
An' I could wad a thousand pounds,
  She wadna say me no.'   5

Lady Margret stan's in her bower door,
  As straight's a willow wan',
An' by it cam the gardener lad,
  Wi a red rose in his han'.   6

'O will ye fancy me, fair maid?
  I pray you, fancy me;
An' among the flowers in my garden
  I'll shape a weed for thee.   7

'The lilies white shall be your smock,
  Becomes your body neist,
An' your stays shall be o the marigolds,
  Wi a red rose in your breist.   8

'Your gown shall be the smelling thyme,
  An' your petticoat camowine,
An' your apron o the soladene:
  Come kiss, sweetheart, an' join.   9

'Your gloves shall be the lockerin clover,
  That grows in yonder wan,
An' I'll stitch them wi the blue blevets,
  That grows among the lawn.   10

'Your shoes shall be o yon red rue,
  That grows in yon garden fine,
An' I'll line them wi the tapetan:
  Come join your love wi mine.'   11

'Since ye hae shaped a weed for me
  Among your summer flowers,
So I shall pay ye back again
  Among the winter showers.   12

13   'The milk-white snow shall be your smock,
        Becomes your body neist,
    An' the coal-black rain shall be your coat,
        Wi a wind-gale in your breist.

14   'The steed that ye shall ride upon
        Shall be the weather snell,
    An' I'll bridle him wi some norlan blasts,
        An' some sharp showers o hail.

15   'The hat that's be upon your head
        Shall be the suthron gray,
    An' when ye come into my sight
        I'd wish ye were away!'

[Ch 237]   56. The Duke of Gordon's Daughter

1   The Duke o' Gordon had three pretty daughters
        Ladies Sarah, Lisbeth, and Jean;
    They wadna stay at Castle Gordon,
        But they are on to bonnie Aberdeen.

2   They hadna been in bonnie Aberdeen
        But a twalmonth and a day,
    Till Lady Jean's fa'en in love wi' Captain Ogilvie,
        And behind him she winna stay.

3   Word's gane to the noble Duke o' Gordon
        In his bed far he lay
    Lady Jean's fa'en in love wi' Captain Ogilvie,
        And behind him she winna stay.

4   Ye saddle to me my steed,
        And see that ye saddle him seen,
    Till I ride to bonnie Aberdeen,
        Tak' my leave o' my daughter Jean.

Fan he cam' to bonnie Aberdeen   5
   And lichtit on the green,
Down cam' Sarah and Lisbeth,
   But gone was her bonnie Lady Jean.

Ye're welcome Sarah and Lisbeth,   6
   Ye're welcome be to me;
But faur is my daughter Jean
   That she's na meetin' me?

Pardon us, honoured father,   7
   Pardon us to-day
Lady Jean's fa'en in love wi' Captain Ogilvie,
   And behind him she wadna stay.

[Duke sent word to his officer to hang Ogilvie; but –]

I winna hang Captain Ogilvie   8
   For counsel or comman',
But I'll take him from being a proud Captain,
   And make him a single man.

[Capt. is willing to bear it for Jean. They are on their way to Castle
Gordon.]

High grew the hills and the mountains,   9
   Cold grew the frost and the snow;
Lady Jean's shoes they were all torn,
   A foot she couldna go.

Oh but I'm weary wanderin'   10
   Oh but my fortune's been bad,
It sets na the Duke o' Gordon's daughter
   To be followin' a sodger lad.

Oh but I'm weary wanderin',   11
   My colour's aye turnin' wan;
It sets na the Duke of Gordon's daughter
   To be followin' a single man.

Dear lovey, do not weary,   12
   Dear lovey, do not think lang,
Once I was a proud Captain,
   For your sake made single man.

13   Dear lovey, do not weary,
        Dear lovey, do not complain,
      I have one crown in my pocket,
        I'll buy for you stockin's and sheen.

14   Gin I war at the bonnie braes o' Foudlan,
        Far mony merry day I hae been,
      I wad go to bonnie Castle Gordon
        Without either stockin's or sheen.

15   Fan they cam' to bonnie Castle Gordon,
        And stood upon the green,
      The porter he cried wi' a loud voice,
        Here comes bonnie Lady Jean.

16   Oot spak the noble Duke o' Gordon,
        An angry man was he,
      Gar bring me in Jeannie Gordon
        But awa wi' him Johnnie Ogilvie!

                *   *   *

17   Mind nae ye Jeannie Gordon
        Fan ye wear the goons o' green
      Ye ware the silken stockins
        But than the satin sheen,
      But noo ye follow Captain Ogilvie
        And your bare soles to the green.

18   Word's cam' to bonnie Captain Ogilvie,
        Trainin' at his men,
      Hoist up sails, Captain Ogilvie,
        Hoist up sails and go hame.
      Hoist up sails, Captain Ogilvie,
        And heir bonnie Northumberlan'.

19   Fat's this, says bonnie Captain Ogilvie,
        That ye tell unto me?
      Far is my brother William?
        He is far nearer than me.

20   Your brother William is dead,
        And to you he's left the lan',
      Hoist up sails, Captain Ogilvie,
        Hoist up sails an' gae hame.

He hadna been at bonnie Northumberlan',   21
   A day but barely three,
Till he'll go to bonnie Castle Gordon
   His bonnie Lady Jean for to see.

Fan he cam' to bonnie Castle Gordon,   22
   And on the green stood he,
The porter he cried wi' a loud voice,
   Here comes Captain Ogilvie.

Doon cam' the noble Duke o' Gordon,   23
   Wi' his gold-laced hat in his han',
Ye're welcome my good son,
   Ye're welcome to the lan'.

I am your good son,   24
   And that I own to be;
But far is my bonnie Lady Jean
   That she's nae meetin' me?

Your Lady Jean's upstairs,   25
   And your young son on her knee,
Come upstairs Captain Ogilvie
   Your bonnie Lady Jean for to see.

Last fan I was at Castle Gordon,   26
   Ye wadna lat me in,
Noo I'm come to bonnie Castle Gordon
   And in I winna come.

Doon cam' his bonnie Lady Jean   27
   Wi her young son in her han'
Ye're welcome, my dear love,
   Ye're welcome to the lan'.

Over the hills and the mountains,   28
   Through cold frost and snow,
Till strong death us part
   Awa' wi' you I'll go.

Over the hills and mountains   29
   Through cold frost to wide,
Go wi' me ye sall never
   In a carriage ye sall ride.

[Ch 240] 57. The Rantin Laddie

*   *   *

1
Oft hae I played at the cards an' the dice
  Wi my ain dear rantin laddie,
But noo I maun sit in my father's kitchie-nook,
  An' sing Ba to my bastard baby.

2
My father dear he knows me not,
  My mother's quite forgot me,
My frien's an' relations they a' slight me,
  An' the servants they do hate me.

3
Gin I had but een o my father's merry men,
  As aft-times I've had mony,
That wad run on to the gates o Aboyne
  Wi a letter to my rantin laddie.

4
'Is your love a laird or is he a lord,
  Or is he but a caddie,
That ye so aft call on his name,
  Your ain dear rantin laddie?'

5
'My love's nae a laird nor is he a lord,
  Nor is he but a caddie,
But he's earl ower a' the lands o Aboyne,
  He's my ain dear rantin laddie.'

6
'Ye sall hae een o your father's merry men
  As aft-times ye've had mony,
That will rin on to the gates o Aboyne
  Wi a letter to your rantin laddie.'

7
Fan he lookit the letter on,
  An' O, but he was sorry:
'O they hae been cruel an' they've been unkind
  To my ain dear rantin lassie.

8
'Her father dear he knows her not,
  Her mother's quite forgot her,
Her frien's an' relations they a' slight her,
  An' the servants they do hate her.

9
'But I will raise an hundred men,
  An' O, but they'll shine bonnie,
An' I'll mount them a' on milk-white steeds
  To bring home my rantin lassie.'

As they rode down thro Buchanshire,   10
  An' Buchanshire shone bonnie;
Rejoice, rejoice, ye Buchan maids a',
  Rejoice an' be na sorry.

Gin ye lay your love on a lowland lad,   11
  He'll do a' he can to slight ye;
Gin ye lay your love on a highland lad,
  He'll do a' he can to raise ye.

58. Young Allan   [*Ch 245*]

When a' the Hawks o Oxenford   1
  Was drinkin at the wine,
There cam a reesin them amon
  In a unseily time.

Some they reesed the Hawk, the Hawk,   2
  An' some o them the Houn',
An' some o them their Comely Cog
  That floated on the faem.

Oot it spak an English knight,   3
  An' a prood word spak he:
'There's nae a ship in Leve London
  That'll sail aboard wi me.'

Then oot it spak a bonnie boy,   4
  Steed by Young Allan's knee:
'My master has a coal car[rier]
  That'll sail aboard wi thee.

'She'll sail ootower the leaf, the leaf,   5
  An' in under the lee,
An' seven times intil a nicht
  She'll tak the win' fae thee.'

'I widna wad nae less wager   6
  Nor twenty tuns o wine,
An' syne as much gweed red scarlet
  As wid cleathe the merrie men.'

7   He to ship an' he to ship,
          An' shippin made them boun',
      There was nae a squire in a' the ships
          Had will to weet their han',
      But I fear or a' the play was ower,
          They wat their golden ban'.

8   There was nae a squire in a' the ships
          Had will to weet their sheen,
      But I fear or a' the play was ower
          Their hats was weet abeen.

9   Allan steed upo the shore,
          Min't him on ill an' gweed,
      'I winna go to ship,' he said,
          'Till I say mess an' dine,
      An' tak my leave o my ladie,
          Go to my gweed ship syne.

10   'Eat an' drink, my merry men a',
          Our gweed ship sails the morn.'
      'Ochone, alas! my dear master,
          It bodes a deadly storm.

11   'The streen I saw the new, new meen
          An' the aul meen in her arms:
      'Ochone, alas! my dear master,
          It bodes a deadly storm.'

12   They hae sailed fae Monanday
          Till Tysday o the nicht,
      An' they hae sailed fae Wednesday
          Till Feersday vera richt

13   An' bonnie was the feather-beds
          Was floatin on the faem,
      But bonnier was the women's sons
          Was sinkin to the san'.

14   'Is there nae a boy in my ship
          Wid tak my helm in han'
      Till I go up to my tapmast
          An' see gin I see lan'?'

'Here am I a bonnie boy   15
    Will tak your helm in han',
But gin ye go up to yon tapmast,
    I fear ye'll never come doon.

'Come here, come here, my master dear,   16
    See ye nae what I see?
For through an' through your comely cog
    I see the green heowe sea,
An' the Black Snake o Leve London,
    I see her blawn by me.

'What wid ye gie, my master dear,   17
    What wid ye gie to me,
That wi the help o my Maker
    Wid bring ye safe fae sea?'

'The half o the ship an' the half o the gear   18
    It's I will gie to thee,
An' my ae sister, Lady Maisry,
    Your wedded wife to be.'

He's taen up a feather-bed   19
    An' wrappit it in aroon,
An' pick't her weel an' spared her not
    An' leet nae water in.

'Is there nae a boy in my ship   20
    Will tak my helm in han',
Till I go up to my tapmast
    An' see gin I see lan'?'

'Here am I a bonnie boy   21
    Will tak your helm in han'
Till ye go up to your tapmast,
    But master, stayna lang.'

The firstan shore that he did see   22
    It was the towers o Lin,
The nextan shore that he did see
    Was bonnie Aberdeen.

'Sail forth, sail forth, my comely cog,   23
    Sail forth against the win',

168

An' the firstan shore that ye come till
   Ye'se get a year's rest in;
A firlot syne a gweed red gowd
   'S be gien at your partin.'

24   The ship she widna go aboot
   Till she heard the heavy meed,
An' syne she sprang oot thro' the waves
   As sparks go fae the gleed.

25   The firstan shore that she cam till
   Was bonnie Aberdeen,
An' the young men lap upo the shore
   Wi their low buckled sheen.

26   'What do ye think, my master dear,
   What do ye think o me,
That wi the help o my Maker
   Has brought ye safe fae sea?'

27   'The half o the ship an' the half o the gear,
   It's I will gie to thee,
An' my ae sister, Lady Maisry,
   Your wedded wife to be;
She may think hersel a happy woman
   The day she does wed thee.'

[Ch 251]   59. Lang Johnny More

1   There lives a lad in Rhynie's lands,
   An' anither on Auchindore,
But the bonniest lad among them a'
   Was lang Johnnie More.
      A riddle a in aldinadie,
      A riddle a in aldinee.

2   Young Johnnie was a clever youth,
   Sturdy, stoot an' strang,
An' the sword that hung by Johnnie's side
   Was fully ten feet lang.

Young Johnnie was a clever youth,   3
    A sturdy, stoot an' wight,
He was full three yards aboot the waist,
    An' fourteen fit o height.

An' if a' be true that they do say,   4
    An' if a' be true we hear
Young Johnnie's on to fair England
    The king's standard to bear.

He hadna been in fair England   5
    A year but barely three,
Till the fairest lady in a' London
    Fell in love wi young Johnnie.

Word's gane up an' word's gane doon   6
    An' word's gane to the king,
That the muckle Scot had fa'en in love
    Wi his daughter, Lady Jean.

'An a' be true that they do say   7
    An' that you tell to me,
That wighty Scot shall strait the rope
    An' hangit he shall be.'

But oot it spoke young Johnnie then,   8
    This words pronouncèd he:
'While I hae strength to wield my blade
    Ye daurna a' hang me.'

But the English dogs is cunnin rogues,   9
    An' roon him they did creep,
They've gien him drams o laudamy,
    Till he fell fast asleep.

Fan Johnnie wauken'd fae his sleep   10
    A sorry man was he,
Wi his jaws an' hands in iron bands
    An' his feet in fetters three.

'Faur will I get a bonnie boy,   11
    That will win baith meat an' fee,
An' will rin on to my uncle
    At the fit o Bennachie?'

12   'O here am I, a bonnie boy,
         That will win baith meat an' fee,
     An' will rin on to your uncle
         At the fit o Bennachie.'

13   'For faur ye fin' the brigs broken,
         Ye'll bend your bow an' swim,
     An' faur ye fin' the grass growin
         Ye'll slack your shoes an' rin.

14   'Fan ye come on to Bennachie
         Ye'll bide neither to chap nor ca',
     Weel will ye ken auld Johnnie there,
         Three fit abeen them a'.

15   'Ye'll gie him this broad letter
         Sealed wi my faith an' troth,
     An' ye'll bid him bring alang wi him
         The body Jock o Noth.'

16   Faur he fan' the brigs broken,
         He bent his bow an' swam,
     An' faur he fan' the grass growin
         He slackit his shoes an' ran.

17   Fan he cam on to Bennachie
         He bade neither to chap nor ca',
     Weel did he ken auld Johnnie there,
         Three fit abeen them a'.

18   'Fat news, fat news, my bonnie boy,
         Ye never was here before?' –
     'Nae news, nae news, but a broad letter
         Fae your nephew Johnnie More.

19   'Ye tak here this broad letter,
         Sealed wi his oath an' troth,
     An' ye're bidden bring alang wi ye
         The body Jock o Noth.'

20   Bennachie lies very low,
         An' the Tap o Noth stands high,
     But for a' the distance that lies atween
         They heard auld Johnnie cry.

Upon the plains the chieftains met,   21
   Twa grizzly guests to see,
They were three fit atween each [?brow],
   An' their shoulders broad yards three.

This men they ran ower hills an' dales,   22
   An' over mountains high,
An' they arrived at fair England
   At the dyin o the day.

When they arrived at fair London   23
   The gates were lockèd in,
An' wha saw they but the trumpeter,
   Wi his trumpet in his han'.

'Fat's the maitter,' auld Johnnie says,   24
   'O fat's the maitter within,
That the drums do beat an' the bells do ring
   An' mak sic a doleful din?'

'Naething's the maitter,' the keeper said,   25
   'Naething's the maitter to thee,
But a wighty Scot's to strait the rope,
   An' tomorrow he maun dee.'

'Open the gates,' auld Johnnie said,   26
   'Open the gates, I say.' –
The tremblin keeper smiled an' said,
   'But we have not the key.'

'Open the gates,' auld Johnnie said,   27
   'Open the gates, I say,
Or there is a body at my back
   Fae Scotland's brought the key.'

'Open the gates,' said Jock o Noth,   28
   'Open them at my call,'
An' wi his fit he has dung in
   Three yard-breadths o the wall.

'Ye may chance to wear us oot,   29
   Or we may chance to fail,
For ye see that we are weighèd doon
   Wi weighty coats o mail.'

30   They are doon thro fair London,
          An' doon by the town hall,
       An' there they saw young Johnnie More
          Stand on the English wall.

31   'Ye're welcome here, my uncle dear,
          Ye're welcome here to me,
       Ye loose the knot an' slack the rope,
          An' take me fae the tree.'

32   'Faur is the lady?' auld Johnnie cried,
          'Sae fain I wad her see,
       For I hae sworn a solemn oath,
          She's go to Bennachie.'

33   'O tak the lady,' the king he says,
          'Ye're welcome to her for me,
       For I never thocht to see sic men
          Fae the fit o Bennachie.'

34   'If I had known,' said Jock o Noth,
          'That ye'd wonder sae much at me,
       I sud hae brocht Sir John o Echt an' Park,
          He's thirty fit an' three.'

35   'But wae betide that little wee boy,
          That tidings brocht to thee;
       Let all England say what they will,
          Sae hangit he shall be.'

36   'O if ye hang that little wee boy
          That tidings brought to me,
       We shall attend the burial,
          An' rewarded ye shall be.'

37   'O tak the lady,' the king he said,
          'Ye're welcome to her for me,
       O tak the lady,' the king he said,
          'An' the boy he shall go free.'

38   'A priest, a priest,' young Johnnie cried,
          'To join my love an' me.'
       'A clerk, a clerk,' the king he cried,
          'To seal her tocher wi.'

But oot it spak auld Johnnie then,   39
   This words pronouncèd he:
'O he has lands an' rents enow,
   An' he'll seek nae gowd fae thee.

'He has lands an' rents enow,   40
   He has thirty ploughs an' three,
Likewise fa's heir to my estate
   At the fit o Bennachie.'

'Hae ye ony masons,' says Jock o Noth,   41
   'Ony at your call,
Hae ye ony masons in this place
   To build up your broken wall?'

'I've plenty masons in this place,   42
   An' plenty at my call,
But ye may from whence ye came,
   Never mind my broken wall.'

They've ta'en the lady by the han',   43
   An' set her prison free;
Wi drums beatin an' fifes playin,
   They're on to Bennachie.

60. The White Fisher   [*Ch 264*]

'It's but a month, my lady gay,   1
   Now since I wedded thee,
Tell me fa's is the bonnie baby
   That I see you go wi?

'O is it to a man o might,   2
   Or a baron o high degree?
Or is it to your father's footpage? –
   My lady, ye dinna lee.'

'It's not to man o might,' she said,   3
   'Or baron o high degree,
But it is to my father's foot-page,
   My good lord, I'll tell thee.

4   'He sair'd my father seven year,
        An' he never paid him nae fee,
     But he got me in a bower my leen,
        An' he made me pay the fee.'

5   Then it fell eence upon a day,
        Her good lord went from home,
     An' heavy heavy were the pains, the pains o
            travailin,
        An' her good lord far from home.

6   She bolted the door without, without,
        She bolted it within,
     She bolted her room round about,
        None to her could come in.

7   Then word is gone to that good lord,
        As he sat drinkin wine,
     Word is gone to that good lord,
        An' merrily cam he home.

8   'Ye open the door, my lady,' he said,
        'Ye open the door to me,
     Or I'll mak a vow an' keep it true,
        In the floor I'll gar it flee.'

9   'I'll open the door, my ain good lord,
        I'll open, lat you come in,
     But all that I do ask o you
        Is that you come in your leen.'

10 But wi her fingers long an' small
        She lifted up the pin,
     An' wi her arms long an' wide
        She embraced her good lord in.

11 'O ye tak up this little boy
        That ye see here wi me,
     O ye tak up this little boy,
        An' throw him in the sea.

12 'An' if he sink ye lat him sink,
        If he swim, ye lat him swim,
     But never lat him return again
        Till fite fish he fess home.'

He's taen up this little boy,   13
   An' he rowed him in his sleeve,
An' he is on to his mother,
   At his lady he asked nae leave.

'Open the door, my mother,' he says,   14
   'Open, lat me come in,
Open the door, my mother,' he says,
   'An tak in my little young son.'

'Didna I tell you, my dear son dear,   15
   When ye was gaun to ride,
Didna I tell you, my dear son dear.
   It was nae leal virgin that ye did wed.'

'O haud your tongue, my mother dear,   16
   Lat a' your folly be,
For I wyte it was a king's daughter
   That sent this boy to me.

'I wyte it was a king's daughter   17
   I loved beyond the sea,
An' gin my lady knew o it,
   Right angry wad she be.'

'Gin that be true, my dear son dear,   18
   As your ain tongue winna lee,
I will tak in your little young son,
   An' gie him a nerice tee.
There will never be waur done to your young son
   Nor ever was done to thee.'

When he came home to his lady,   19
   An' sair mournin was she,
'O what does ail my gay lady,
   I pray you tell to me?'

'O bonnie was the fite fisher   20
   That I sent to the sea;
Lang will I mourn in bower my leen
   Ere fite fish come to me.'

'O haud your tongue, my gay lady,   21
   Lat a' your mournin be,
There'll never be waur done to your young son
   Nor ever was done to thee.'

22   'Gin that be true, my ain dear lord,
        This day noo well is me;
     But gin it hadna come o you,' she says,
        'It never wad come o me.

23   'My blessin on your cheek, your cheek,
        My blessin on your chin,
     My blessin on your red rose lips,
        For ye're aye a woman's frien'.'

[Ch 274]   61. Our Goodman

1   Hame cam oor gudeman at e'en,
        An hame cam he,
     An' there he saw a saddle horse
        Faur nae horse should be.
     'O how cam this horse,
        How can this be?
     How cam this horse here
        Without the leave o me?'

2   'Ye aul blin' doited body,
        Blin'er mat ye be,
     It's but a bonnie milk cow
        My mammie sent to me.' –
     'Far hae I ridden,
        An' muckle hae I seen,
     But saddles upon milk kye
        Saw I never neen.'

3   Oor gudeman cam hame at e'en,
        An' hame cam he,
     An' there he spied a pair o boots
        Faur nae boots should be.
     'Fat's this, or fa's is't,
        An' fa's may it be?
     An' foo cam this boots here
        Without the leave o me?'

4   'Ye aul blin' doited body,
        Unco blin', I see,

It's but a pair o water stoups
  My mammie sent to me.' –
'Far hae I ridden,
  An' muckle hae I seen,
But siller spurs on water stoups
  Saw I never neen.'

Our gudeman cam hame at e'en   5
  An' hame cam he,
An' there he saw a sillert gun
  Faur nae gun should be.
'Fat's this, or fa's is't,
  Or fa's mat it be?
An' foo cam this gun here
  Without the leave o me?'

'Ye aul blin' doited body,   6
  Blin'er mat ye be,
It's but a bonnie spurtle
  My mammie sent to me.' –
'Far hae I ridden,
  An' far hae I been
But siller-mounted spurtles
  Saw I never neen.'

Hame cam oor gudeman at e'en,   7
  An' hame cam he,
An' there he saw a feathered cap
  Faur nae cap should be.
'Fat's this or fa's is't,
  An' fa's may it be?
An' foo cam this cap here
  Without the leave o me?'

'Ye aul blin' doited body,   8
  Blin'er may ye be,
It's but a tappit clockin hen
  My minnie sent to me.' –
'Far hae I ridden,
  An' muckle hae I seen,
But fite cockades on clockin hens
  Saw I never neen.'

9
    Ben the hoose gaed oor gudeman,
      An' ben gaed he,
    An' there he saw a hielan plaid
      Faur nae plaid should be.
    'Fat's this or fa's is't,
      Or fa's mat it be?
    An' foo cam this plaid here
      Without the leave o me?'

10
    'Heely, heely noo, gudeman,
      An' dinna angry be,
    It cam wi cousin Macintosh
      Fae the north countrie.'
    'Your cousin,' quo he;
      'Ay, my cousin,' quo she.
    'Blin' may ye jibe me,
      I've sight enough to see
    Ye're hidin rebels in the hoose
      Without the leave o me.'

10a
    ['We'll a be hang'd an' quarter'd,
      An' that ye'll seen see,
    For hidin rebels in the hoose
      Without the leave o me.']

11
    Hame cam oor gudeman at e'en,
      An' hame cam he,
    He gat a man in the bed
      Faur nae man should be.
    'Fat's this or fa is't,
      Or fa mat it be?
    An' foo cam this man here
      Without the leave o me?'

12
    'Ye aul blin' doited body
      Blin'er mat ye be,
    It's but a bonnie milkmaid
      My mammie sent to me.' –
    'Far hae I ridden,
      An' muckle hae I seen,
    But beards upon milkmaids
      Saw I never neen.'

62. Get Up and Bar the Door [Ch 275]

It fell aboot a Martimas time,   1
  An' a fine time it was than,
That oor gudewife got puddens to mak,
  An' she boiled them in a pan.
    An' the barrin o oor door, weel, weel, weel,
      An the barrin o oor door, weel.

The wind it blew fae to east to west,   2
  An' blew upon the floor,
Says oor gudeman to oor gudewife,
  'Get up an' bar the door.'

'My han' is in my hissy-skip,   3
  Gudeman, as ye may see;
Though it sudna be barred this seven year,
  It's nae to be barred by me.'

They made a paction 'tween themsels,   4
  An' fixed it firm an' sure,
That the een wha spoke the foremost word
  Sud rise an' bar the door.

Twa gentlemen had lost their road   5
  At twal o'clock at nicht,
An' they cudna [   ] hoose nor hall,
  Nor coal nor candle-licht.

      *   *   *

First they ate the fite pudden,   6
  An' syne they ate the black,
An' oor gudeman said to himsel,
  'The deil gae doon wi that.'

The young man to the aul' man said,   7
  'Here, man, tak ye my knife,
An' gang an' shave the gudeman's beard,
  An' I'll kiss the gudewife.'

'There is no water in the hoose,   8
  An' fat'll we do than?'
'Fat ails ye at the pudden-bree
  That boils into the pan?'

9   Then oot it spak the aul' gudeman,
            An' an angry man was he:
        'Wad ye kiss my wife afore my een?
            Scaud me wi pudden bree?'

10   Then up it raise the aul' gudewife,
            Gae three skips on the floor:
        'Gudeman, ye spoke the foremost word,
            Get up an' bar the door.'

[*Ch 277*] 63. The Wife Wrapt in Wether's Skin

1   There was an aul cooper lived in Fife, –
            Nickity, nackity, noo, noo –
        An' he has gotten a gentle wife –
            Sing, Hey Willie Wallachie, how John Dugal,
        Alane, quo' Rushitie rue, rue, rue.

2   She wadna wash an' she wadna wring, etc.,
        For fear o spoilin her gowden ring, etc.

3   She wadna card an' she wadna spin, etc.,
        For fear o shamin her gentle kin, etc.

4   He's done him up to the sheep's faul', etc.,
        An' catcht a wedder by the spaul, etc.

5   An' he's ta'en aff the wedder's skin, etc.,
        An' rowed the dainty lady in, etc.

6   'I manna thrash ye for your gentle kin,' etc.,
        'But weel may I leather my ain sheep's skin,' etc.

The Modern Tradition (ii): The Bothy Ballads

64. The Hireman Chiel

1 There was a knight and a baron bright,
  And a bold baron was he;
 And he had only but one son,
  And a comely youth was he.

2 He brought him up at schools nine,
  So did he at schools ten;
 And the boy learned to hold the plough
  Amongst his father's men.

3 But it fell once upon a day
  The bold baron did say –
 You will go, my son, and get some dame
  To share this gifts with thee.

4 It's you have lands and rents [he said]
  You have castles and turrets three;
 You will go, my son, and get some dame
  To share that gifts with thee.

5 It's I have lands and rents, father,
  I have castles and toors three;
 But if she loved my lands and rents
  Mair nor she loved me.

6 But I will go and get a wife
  That well can please my eye;
 But I will fairly try her love
  Before she goes with me.

7 He has ta'en off the jockey coat
  Bedecked with shining gold;
 And he put on the hireman's coat
  Till keep him from the cold.

8 He took a stick intill his hand
  That he could bravely wiel';
 And he's gane whistlin' o'er the hill
  Like ony hireman chiel.

9 He gaed up yon high high hill,
  And low in yonder glen;
 And there he spied a gay castle,
  With turrets nine or ten.

As he gaed on and farther on,   10
   Till to the yett drew he,
And there he spied a weel far'd maid
   That pleased that young man's e'e.

Straight he went to the grieve's chamber,   11
   And with humility –
O hae ye ony kind o' wark
   For a hireman loon like me?

What is the wark ye tak' in han',   12
   Or how can we agree?
Can you reap, plough, and sow the corn,
   An' a' for meat and fee?

Yes, I can plough, reap, mow and sow,   13
   And sow your corn tee;
An' I can well manage horse and cows,
   An' a' for meat an' fee.

Gin ye can haud the plough richt weel,   14
   An' sow the corn tee,
By faith an' troth, my hireman loon,
   We sanna pairt for fee.

He put his hand in his pocket,   15
   He's taen out shillings nine –
Says, Tak' ye that, my hireman loon,
   An' turn ye in an' dine.

I acted all I took in han',   16
   His master loved him weel;
But that young lady in the lan'
   Fell in love wi' the hireman chiel.

For oft she tried to drown her flame   17
   She oft wept bitterly;
But aye she loved her hireman loon,
   Sae weel's he pleased her e'e.

She wrote to him a broad letter,   18
   And seal't it with her han',
And dropt it at the stable door,
   Where this young man did stan.

19 I am in love, my hireman loon,
       I'm deep in love wi' thee,
    An' if you think me worth your love,
       In the garden green meet me.

20 When he had read that letter o'er,
       A loud, loud laugh gaed he,
    Says, if I manage my business weel,
       I'm sure to get my fee.

21 Next morning by the rising sun,
       She, wi' her Marys fair,
    Walk'd through the field to see the plough,
       An' meet her hireman there.

22 Good morn, good morn, my lady gay;
       I wonder much at you,
    To rise so early in a morn,
       While fields are wet wi' dew.

23 I wonder much at you, young man,
       I wonder much at you,
    That you no other station have,
       Than hold my father's plough.

24 I love as weel to rise each morn
       As you can your Maries fair;
    I love as weel to hold the plough
       As though I were your father's heir.

25 If you love as you protest,
       As I trust that ye do,
    The morn's night at eight o'clock
       In good green wood meet me.

26 Yes, I love you, my hireman loon,
       An' that most tenderly;
    But if you wrong'd my virgin honour,
       Slighted I would be.

27 Tak' ye no dread, my bonnie lass,
       Lat a' your folly be;
    If you come a maiden to green wood,
       You'll return the same for me.

It was a dark and dismal night,   28
  No stars blink'd o'er the lea,
When the lassie and her hireman met
  Beneath yon spreading tree.

The laddie took her in his arms,   29
  Embraced her tenderly;
An' thrice he kiss'd her rosy lips,
  Beneath yon greenwood tree.

Haud aff your hands, young man, she said,   30
  I wonder much at thee, –
The man that holds my father's plough
  Would lay his hands on me.

No harm I mean, my pretty dame,   31
  No impudence at a';
I never laid my hands on you
  Till your liberty I saw.

But morn it is coming in,   32
  The dew is falling down,
An' you must go home again,
  Or spoil your satin gown.

If ye are wearied with me so soon,   33
  Why did ye tryst me here?
I would not weary with you, my dear,
  Though this night were a year.

When morning sun began to peep   34
  Amang the branches green,
These lovers rose to part to meet
  To tell their tale again.

I will go home unto the plough,   35
  Where I have often been;
I'll tak' my mantle folded up,
  Walk in the garden green.

The baron and my mother dear   36
  Will wonder what I mean;
They'll think I am disturbed sair,
  When I am up sae seen.

37   [But] this past [on], and farther on,
          Till two months and a day,
      Till word came to the bold baron,
          Then an angry man was he.

38   The baron swore a solemn oath,
          An angry man was he, –
      The more before I eat or drink
          High hanged he shall be.

39   O woe is me, the lady said;
          O do not troubled be, –
      Whene'er they touch a hair of your head,
          They'll get no good of me.

40   He turn'd him right an' roun' about,
          An' a loud, loud laugh gaed he, –
      A man stood never in a court
          That daur this day hang me.

41   Her mother stood in the bower door,
          And an angry woman was she, –
      What impudence it was in you
          To tryst her to the greenwood tree.

42   An' she hadna gi'en her consent,
          She had never ga'en wi' me;
      You may wed your daughter when you will,
          For she's none the worse of me.

43   He turn'd him right an' roun' about,
          A loud, loud laugh gaed he, –
      If she's gane a maiden to greenwood,
          She return'd the same for me.

44   He's gone whistlin' o'er the knowe,
          Swift as a bird that flew;
      But the lassie stood in her bower door,
          An' lat the saut tears fa'.

45   But this pass'd on and farther on,
          Till two months and a day,
      There came a knight and a baron bright
          To woo this lady gay.

Soon he gain'd the baron's will,   46
    Likewise her mother gay;
He woo'd and won that lady's love,
    But by a slow degree.

O well befa' you, daughter dear,   47
    An' aye well may you be,
To lay your love on that grand knight,
    An' lat the hireman be.

O hold your tongue, my father dear,   48
    An' say not so to me;
For more I love yon hireman loon
    Than a' the knights I see.

The morn came, and bells were rung,   49
    An' a' to church repair;
An' like a rose among the thorns
    Was the lady and her maidens fair.

But as they walked across the field   50
    Among the flowers sae fair,
Beneath a tree stood on the plain
    A hireman loon was there.

I wish you well, my madam gay,   51
    An' aye well may ye be;
For here's a ring, a pledge of love,
    That ance I got frae thee.

O wae befa' you, hireman loon,   52
    Some ill death may ye dee;
Ye might hae tell't to me your name,
    Your hame and your country.

If ye love me as ye protest,   53
    As I trust that ye do,
You'll turn your love from this brave knight,
    And reach your hand to me.

It's out it spake the gay baron,   54
    And an angry man was he, –
If I had known she was beloved,
    She'd never been loved by me.

55   When she was on his high horse back,
       An' postin' thro' the glen,
    She saw her father followin' fast
       Wi' fifty armed men.

56   As they gaed up yon high high hill,
       An' low down in yon glen,
    They saw his father's gilded coach
       Wi' five hundred gentlemen.

57   Turn back, turn back, my hireman loon,
       Turn back and speak wi' me;
    You've served me lang for my daughter's sake,
       Your hame and your country.

58   Your blessin' give me instantly,
       It's all I'll crave of thee;
    Seven years I served for her sake,
       But now I've got my fee.

65. The Barnyards o Delgaty

1   In New Deer parish I was born,
       A child in youth to Methlick came;
    And if you doubt me to believe
       The session-clerk will tell the same.

Ref.   Lintin adie toorin adie,
       Lintin adie toorin ae.

2   Good education I did get
       And I did learn to read and write,
    My parents they did me admire
       My mother I was her whole delight

3   But as the years they did roll on,
       My dad and me could not agree,
    I loved the lasses double weel,
       And aye the drap o' barley bree.

Fae Methlick parish I cam' fae   4
   To Turra market for to fee,
When I met in wi' drucken Scott
   Fae the Barnyards o' Delgaty

When I arrived at the Barnyards,   5
   The sicht o' things near upset me,
We had nae tools to work oor wark,
   Oor beddin' it was unco wee.

Oor cairts they were all in a wrack,   6
   Oor harrows scarce a teeth ava;
Oor ploos they were a lump o' roost,
   And handles they had nane ava.

Oor horses they were unco thin,   7
   The auld gray meer she widna ca;
The auld Jock horse lay in the theets,
   And clawed his legs in spite o' a'

But when the turnips we got in,   8
   Oor horse a' parkit ane an' a';
And we to Turriff on Saturday went,
   And jolly we got ane an' a'.

When I went to the church on Sunday,   9
   Mony's the bonnie lass I see,
Sit shyly by her daddie's side,
   And winkin' owre the pews to me.

I can drink and nae be drunk,   10
   I can fight and nae be slain,
I can coort my neebor's lass,
   And aye be welcome to my ain.

66. Drumdelgie

There's a farmie up in Cairnie,   1
   That's kent baith far and wide,
Tae rise i' the mornin' early
   Upon sweet Deveronside.

2   At five o'clock we quickly rise,
        And hurry doon the stair,
    To get oor horses a' weel corned,
        Likewise to straught their hair.

3   Then after that we usher oot
        Intae the kitchen goes,
    To get some breakfast for oorsels,
        Which is generally brose.

4   We've scarcely got oor brose weel supped,
        And gien oor pints a tie,
    When the gaffer shouts, 'Hallo, my lads,
        The hour is drawin' nigh.'

5   The mill gaes on at sax o'clock,
        To gie us a strait wark,
    And sax o' us we mak' to her
        Or ye could wring oor sark.

6   And when the water is put aff,
        We hurry doon the stair,
    To get some quarters thro' the fan,
        Till daylight does appear.

7   When daylight it begins to dawn,
        The sky begins to clear,
    The gaffer shouts 'Hallo my lads,
        You'll stay nae langer here.'

8   There's sax o' you'll gae to the plough,
        And twa can ca the neeps,
    And the oxen they'll be after you,
        Wi' stray raips roon their queets.

9   Oh when we a' were gyaun oot,
        And drivin' oot tae yoke,
    The snaw dang on sae thick and fast,
        That we were like to choke.

10   Oor horses bein' but young and sma'
        The shafts wid hardly fill,
    And aften not the saddler lad
        To pit them up the hill.

But we will sing oor horses' praise,   11
    Though they be young and sma',
For they mak' a feel o' their neiper toons,
    That gang sae bonnie and braw.

Sae fare ye weel, Drumdelgie,   12
    For I maun gang awa',
Sae fare ye weel, Drumdelgie,
    Your weety weather and a'.

Fare ye weel, Drumdelgie,   13
    I bid you all adieu
I leave ye as I got ye –
    A damned unceevil crew.

67. John Bruce o the Forenit

Ae Martmas term I gaed to the fair,   1
    To view the sweet lassies and sniff the fresh air,
And fee'd wi' a mannie to ca' his third pair,
    And his name's Johnnie Bruce o' the Forenit.

Fin I gaed hame tae this man John Bruce,   2
    He lived o'er at Skene in a blue sklaitet hoose,
A guid hertit mannie but he lookit some cross,
    Fin I gaed hame tae the Forenit.

The first Sunday morning were tempered at ease,   3
    Fin oot cam' auld Johnnie wi' a flagon o' grease,
Tae rub oor horse legs fra the queets tae the knees,
    They're a' cripple nags at the Forenit.

The heat o' the horse syne melted the grease,   4
    An oot there cam' a swarm o' fleas,
Says we tae oorsels it's the Plague o' the Fleas
    Sent doon on the lads at the Forenit.

Here's tae oor Gaffer, a cannie auld man,   5
    He'll neither swear at ye, curse nor damn,
There's nae aneuch o' the deevil in him
    For auld Johnnie Brisee o' the Forenit.

6   Here's tae oor foreman, he comes frae Balquine,
         His name is McGilvry, he wrocht on the line,
      He meats his horse weel, bit he hauds on the twine,
         For the wark's aye ahin' at the Forenit.

7   Here's tae oor second lad, a sturdy young chiel,
         He sticks tae his wark and it sets him richt weel,
      But he wisna lang hame fin he seen seemed to yield
         Tae auld Johnnie Brice o' the Forenit.

8   Here's tae oor third's man tae rant and tae reel
         Some half o' a poet, some half o' a feel,
      But the lasses are roon him they like him sae weel
         That he'll seen hae tae gang frae the Forenit.

9   Here's tae oor baillie, he comes frae Kinnaird,
         A little wee mannie and scant o' a beard,
      For coortin the lasses he aye seems prepared
         And sortin his stots at the Forenit

10   The loon he wis feed tae advance and retire
         Atween the neep park an the auld coo byre,
      But he wisna lang hame fin he seen seemed to tire
         Wi auld Johnnie Brice o' the Forenit.

11   Here's tae oor dochter, the Rose o' the Lane,
         She plays the piano, and whyles wi' the men,
      She gaes thro' the close rinnin tae be keepit again
         By the rovin' young lads o' the Forenit.

12   On Sunday tae the kirk she wears a fite veil,
         And a yaird o' her goon ahin her does trail,
      An her hair tied up like my horse tail,
         Tae charm the lads at the Forenit.

13   The weather bein' bad, and the hairst bein late,
         Ae fine Sunday mornin' a ruckie we led,
      The rest o' the day we gid tae oor bed,
         An prayed for oor sins at the Forenit.

14   The hairst bein' deen and the weather bein bad,
         We wis a' turned oot wi' a pick and a spad,
      He tore aff his jacket, the auld nickum gaed mad,
         Hurrah for John Bruce o' the Forenit.

68. Swaggers

Come all ye gallant heroes,   1
   I pray you'll have a care;
Beware o' meetin Swaggers,
   He'll be in Porter Fair.

He'll be aye [lauch-] lauchin',   2
   He'll be aye lauchin' there;
And he'll hae on the blithest face
   In a' Porter Fair.

Wi' his fine horse and harness,   3
   Sae weel's he'll gar ye true;
But if you come to Auchterless,
   So sair's he'll gar ye rue.

He'll be aye fret-freetin',   4
   He'll be aye frettin' there;
And he'll gie you regulations
   That's worn threadbare.

He will tell you o' some plooin' match 5
   That's nae owre far awa
And gin ye clean yer harness boys
   Yer sure to beat them a'.

For the tackle's gained the prize before 6
   At every country show;
And if you do lat it fall back,
   You'll be thocht little o'.

There's a pair o' blues that leads the van, 7
   So nimbly as they go;
A pair o' browns that follows them,
   That never yet said no.

A wee bit shalt that ca'as the neeps, 8
   An' o' but it is sma';
It's Swaggers will declare to you
   It's stronger than them a'.

But Swaggers in the harvest time,   9
   Will have too much ado
To two three o' the jovial lads
   That drives his cart and ploo.

10   But he'll gang on some twenty [miles],
          Where people doesna him ken;
      And he'll engage some harvest hands,
          And bring them far frae hame.

11   He will tell them a fine story,
          How little is to do;
      And getting them for little fee
          Is a his pride, I true.

12   He'll be aye laugh, laughing,
          He'll be aye laughing there;
      And he'll hae on the blithest face
          In a' Porter Fair.

13   He will say unto the foremost man,
          Keep aye the eident grin,
      And dinna lat the orra lads
          Stan' idle at the end.

14   For I pay you all good wages,
          And so you must go on
      And when you are not able
          There's another when you're done.

15   He will say unto the girlies,
          When they are going back
      Step hardy up my girlies
          Gie them nae time to sharp.

16   But now the cuttin's over,
          And we must try to lead
      And mony the curious plan he'll try
          For to come muckle speed.

17   But syne the wind and rain comes on,
          And dabbles a' our stooks,
      And we must run from field to field,
          For to get them replaced.

18   And when that we go to the raipes,
          He'll get up wi a brawl,
      Play in the twine my girlies,
          You're sure to beat them a'.

But now the sheaves are all got in
  And formed in the stack;
And syne the windy days are come,
  When we must hunt the brock.
19

When we must hunt the brock, my boys,
  Wi' mony a frown and fret;
And Swaggers cries, Come on, my lads
  It's like for to be wet.
20

But now the thack is all put on,
  The rucks have got a snod,
The harvest hands wi' bundles big
  When they must haud the road.
21

They must pad the road, my boys,
  And wander through the snow,
And they hae sworn a solemn oath,
  They'll ne'er come back ava.
22

Martmas it will be here,
  My fee into my pouch;
So merrily as I will sing, Gin I
  Were oot o' the tyrant's clutch.
23

For he is the baddest master
  That ever I did serve;
And if ye'll no believe me,
  Ne'er mind my observe.
24

69. Johnnie Sangster

Of a' the seasons o' the year
  When we maun work the sairest
The harvest is the foremost time,
  And yet it is the rarest.
We rise as seen as mornin' licht,
  Nae craters can be blyther;
We buckle on our finger-steels,
  And follow oot the scyther.
1

Cho. – For you, Johnnie, you, Johnnie
    You Johnnie Sangster,
I'll trim the gavel o' my sheaf,
    For ye're a gallant bandster.

2   A mornin' piece to line oor cheek,
      Afore that we gae forder,
Wi' cloods o' blue tobacco reek
      We then set oot in order.
The sheafs are risin' fast and thick,
      And Johnnie he maun bind them,
The busy group, for fear they stick
      Can scarcely look behind them.
      Cho. –

3   I'll gie you bands that winna slip,
      I'll plait them weel and thraw them
I'm sure they winna tine the grip,
      Hooever weel ye draw them.
I'll lay my leg oot owre the shafe
      And draw the band sae handy.
Wi' ilka strae as straucht's a rash,
      And that'll be the dandy.
      Cho. –

4   Some complain on hacks and thraws,
      And some on brods and bruises,
And some complain on grippet hips
      And stiffness in their troosers;
But as soon as they lay doon the scythe
      The pipers yoke their blawvin,
And in a hint the rabble rook
      They're owre the lugs wi' [tyawvin].
      Cho. –

5   Oh lazy wives they hinna skeel,
      For a their fine pretences,
They'll gar ye trow they're never well,
      And loll upon their hinches.

They sair themsels afore the lave
  Wi a'thing in profusion,
And syne preten' they canna ate,
  Their stammacks hisna fushion.
    Cho. –

If e're it chance to be my lot   6
  To get a gallant bandster,
I'll gar him wear a gentle coat,
  And bring him gowd in hanfu's,
But Johnnie, he can please himsel'
  I widna wish him blinket;
Sae aifter he has brewed his ale,
  He can sit doon and drink it.
    Cho. –

A dainty cowie in the byre,   7
  For butter and for cheeses;
A grumphy feedin' in the stye
  Wad keep the hoose in greases.
A bonnie ewie in the bucht
  Wad help to creesh the ladle;
And we'll get tufts o' cannie woo'
  Wad help to theek the cradle.
    Cho. –

70. Harrowing Time

Cauld winter it is now awa',   I
  And spring has come again;
And the cauld dry winds o' March month
  Has driven awa' the rain;

Has driven awa' the dreary rain,   2
  Likewise the frost and snow;
So our foreman in the morning
  He's ordered out to sow.

3   Then the rest o' us merry ploughboys
       We a' maun follow fast;
     We are told by our hard master
       There is no time to rest.

4   We're told that we must be ayock
       Each morning sharp by five;
     And quickly ower and ower the rigs
       Our horses we must drive.

5   We drive them on till twelve o'clock,
       Syne hame to dinner go;
     And before the end of one hour
       The farmer cries, 'Hillo!'

6   Till the farmer cries, 'Hillo, boys,
       It's time to yoke again;
     See that ye get it harrit oot,
       For fear that it comes rain.'

7   So on we drive until the sun
       Ahint yon hill does hide;
     And syne we lowse our horses tired,
       And homewards we do ride.

8   Then homewards we do ride foo keen,
       To get our horses fed;
     We kaim them weel, baith back and heel,
       Their tails and manes we redd.

9   When that is done we supper get,
       And after that we hie
     Awa' to see our pretty girls,
       Amilkin' o' their kye, –

10   Each to see his pretty girlie
       And pree her cherry mou',
     Then tak' a flaffin' 'oor or twa,
       Shak' hands and bid adieu.

11   So now I mean to end my song,
       And I will end it this, –
     May the ploughman get more wages,
       That is my earnest wish.

That is my heartfelt wish, I say, 12
   It is the ploughman's due;
For he sustains both rich and poor
   By the sweat o' his broo.

71. The Tarves Rant

Give ear to me ye gay young lads, 1
   That means to take a spree,
I'll tell to you a story,
   Withoot ae word o' lee.
It happened once upon a time,
   To Tarves we did go,
To have a spree and hae some fun,
   The truth I'll let you know.

My name I needna mention, 2
   It's hardly worth my while,
I dinna mean to ruin mysel
   Or spend my time in jail.
For I canna work your horses,
   I canna haud your ploo
Cut nor build in harvest,
   But I can feed a coo.

To Tarves we for treacle came, 3
   We bein' on oor brose,
Some o' them for boots and shoes,
   And some o' them for clothes.
There was as few there that I did know
   And as few there knew me,
But there was one amongst the rest
   Who tried to bully me.

When we arrived in Tarves 4
   To Duthie's we did part,
'Twas there we heard fine music
   Which filled our hearts with glad.

The man that played the music,
  His name I winna hide,
He was a gallant ploughboy,
  They ca'd him Ironside.

5   Away to Philip's we did go,
  To have a little fun;
'Twas there I got ensnarèd
  With the maiden o' the inn.
She was a lovely maiden,
  Gey maiden that she be,
Twa rosy cheeks, twa rollin eyes,
  And a lovely maid was she.

6   Drink it was right merriment,
  And drink I think nae shame,
But syne we left the tavern
  To steer oor course for hame.
'Twas there I lost my comrades,
  And on them I did cry,
And at that very moment
  A man in blue cam' by.

7   He told me very quickly,
  If I didn't hold my tongue,
He would take me into custody
  And that before nae lang.
He roughly took me by the arm,
  And dragged me to the inn,
'Twas there we fought right earnestly
  For it didn't end in fun.

8   But surely I'm a profligant,
  A villain to the bone,
To tear the coat frae aff his back,
  And it nae bein' his ain.
[He] tried to shove me in the room,
  His strength he didna spare,
But I could plainly show him
  That it would tak' a pair.

9   But soon assistants they did come,
  And shoved me thro' the door,

And I bein' left a prisoner,
  A prisoner to think o'er.
But such a thocht cam' in my mind
  That I up the window drew;
Twa willin' hands they pulled me oot,
  But I didna like the blue.

I think you folk in Tarves   10
  A jail will need to get,
For to lock up your prisoners
  And nae lat them escape.
For surely it's an awfu' crime
  To brak the Sabbath day,
When searchin for your prisoners
  When they have run away.

A few mair words I'll tell to thee,   11
  It's nae to my disgrace,
They brocht me up to Aiberdeen
  To mak' me plead my case.
But when I heard my sentence,
  I heard it like a shot,
There was thirty shillin's o' a fine,
  And fifteen for his coat.

72. M'Ginty's Meal-an-Ale

This is nae a sang o' love, na, nor yet a sang o' money,
It's naething very peetyfu', an' naething very funny;
But there's Heelan' Scotch, Lowlan' Scotch, Butter Scotch
  an' honey;
  If there's nane o' them for a', there's a mixter o' the
  three.
An' there's nae a word o' beef-brose, sowens, sautie
  bannocks,
Nor o' pancakes an' pess eggs for them wi' dainty stammacks –
It's a' aboot a meal-an'-ale that happen't at Balmannocks,
  M'Ginty's meal-an'-ale far the pig gaed there tae see.

Chorus

They war howlin' in the kitchen like a caravan o' tinkies,
An' some wis playin' ping-pong, an' tiddley-widdley-winkies;
Up the howe or doon the howe there never wis sic jinkies
   As M'Ginty's meal-an'-ale far the pig gaed there tae see.

M'Ginty's pig had broken lowse, an' wan'ert tae the lobby,
Far he open shiv't the pantry door, an' cam' upo' the toddy,
An' he gaed kin'ly tae the stuff, like ony human body,
   At M'Ginty's meal-an'-ale far the pig gaed there tae see.
Miss M'Ginty she ran butt the hoose, the road wis dark an'
   crookit,
She fell heelster-gowdy ower the pig, for it she never lookit,
An' she leet oot a skyrl wid a' paralyst a teuchit,
   At M'Ginty's meal-an'-ale far the pig gaed there tae see.

Chorus

Young Murphy he ran aifter her, an' ower the pig wis leapin',
But he trampit on an ashet that wis sittin' fu' o' dreepin',
An' he fell doon an' peel't his croon, an' couldna haud fae
   greetin',
   At M'Ginty's meal-an'-ale far the pig gaed there tae see.
For the pantry skyelf cam' ricklin' doon, an' he wis lyin'
   kirnin'
Amon' saft soap, piz-meal, corn floor, an' yirnin',
Like a gollach amon' tricle, but M'Ginty's wife wis girnin'
   At the soss upon her pantry fleer, an' widna lat 'im be.

Chorus

Syne they a' ran skyrlin' tae the door, bit fan' that it wis
   tuggit,
For aye it heeld the faister aye the mair they ruggit;
Tull M'Ginty roar't tae bring an aix, he widna be humbuggit,
   Na, nor lockit in his ain hoose, an' that he'd lat them see.
Sae the wife cam' trailin' wi' an aix, an' throu' the bar wis
   hacket,
An' open flew the door at aince, sae close as they war packet,
An' a' the crew gaed tum'lin' oot like tatties fae a backet,
   At M'Ginty's meal-an'-ale far the pig gaed there tae see.

Chorus

They hid spurtles, they hid tatie chappers, troth they warna
  jokin',
An' they said they'd gar the pig claw far he wis never yokin';
Bit be this time the lad wis fou an' didna care a dokin,
  At M'Ginty's meal-an'-ale far the pig gaed there tae see.
O there's eely pigs, an' jeely pigs, an' pigs for haudin'
  butter,
Aye, bit this pig wis greetin' fou an' tum'lin' in the gutter,
Tull M'Ginty an' his foreman trail't 'im oot upon a shutter
  Fae M'Ginty's meal-an'-ale, far the pig gaed there tae see.

Chorus

Miss M'Ginty took the thing tae he'rt an' hidet in her closet,
An' they rubbit Johnny Murphy's heed wi turpenteen an' roset,
An' they harl't him wi' meal an' ale, ye really wid suppose't
  He hid sleepit in a mason's troch, an' risen tae the spree.
O weary on the barley bree, an' weary fa' the widder;
For it's keegerin' amon' dubs an' drink they gyang na weel
  thegidder,
But there's little doot M'Ginty's pig is wishin' for anidder
  O' M'Ginty's meal-an'-ales far the pig gaed there tae see.

Chorus

Tunes

I

[Ch 5] 1. Gil Brenton

Ritson-Tytler-Brown MS., pp. 22-30. Sung by Mrs Brown, Falkland;
copied by Joseph Ritson, *c.* 1792-4.

Mrs Brown's tune, conjectural reading.

a Æ/D

2. Willie's Lady [Ch 6]

Mrs Brown's tune, conjectural reading.

p I/Ly (−II) (compass of sixth)

[O . .] He's woo'd her for her yel - low

hair But's moth - er wrought her mei - - kle care

[*Ch 10*]   ## 3. The Twa Sisters

Mrs Brown's tune, conjectural reading.

m M

There was twa sis - ters in ae bour

Ed - in brough Ed - in - brough, There was twa sis ters

in ae bour Stir - - ling for aye There was

twa sis - ters in ae bour There came a knight to be their woo'r

Bon - ny St. John - ston stands up - on Tay

4. King Henry [*Ch 32*]

a Æ (+ VI in grace note)

8. Young Bekie [*Ch 53C*]

Probably a I, ending on V

[*Ch 65A*]   11. Lady Maisry

a Bimodal? (Æ—Ph)
1st half lacks II (Æ/Ph); 2nd half inflected II and VI and lacks IV, V

[*Ch 96*]   17. The Gay Goshawk

p M (−IV) (or a D, −VII)

MS. READING

CONJECTURALLY THUS

18. Brown Robin [*Ch 97*]

a π^1

MS. READING

CONJECTURAL READING

[Ch 99]   19. Johnie Scot

a Æ

* *Original ending:*

This tune has a bi-modal feeling, the first half seeming to be p I/Ly.

20. Willie o Douglas Dale [*Ch 101*]

m M (unless a I, ending on V)

MS. READING

CONJECTURAL TIMING

[Ch 103]   21. Rose the Red and White Lily

a π³

MS. READING

CORRECTED READING

II

Pat Shuldham-Shaw, the editor of the Greig-Duncan MSS., has copied these tunes from the Greig MSS. and provided the musical notes.

64. As the only informant to supply both text and tune gave just a fragmented text, the song is represented by the substantial text of Mrs Sim and this tune from J. McAllan, Shevado. Most of the tunes recorded for this song in the Greig MSS. are versions of McAllan's.

The Hireman Chiel

from J. McAllan, Shevado.
9/07.

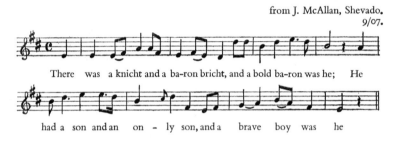

There was a knicht and a ba-ron bricht, and a bold ba-ron was he; He
had a son and an on - ly son, and a brave boy was he

65. On the evidence of the MSS., J. Mowat's tune is pretty much the standard version; it differs from the usual Folk Club version in the chorus.

The Barnyards o Delgaty

from J. Mowat, Craigmaud,
New Pitsligo, 9/07

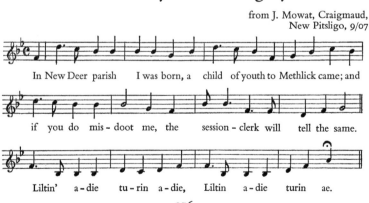

In New Deer parish I was born, a child of youth to Methlick came; and
if you do mis - doot me, the session - clerk will tell the same.
Liltin' a - die tu - rin a - die, Liltin a - die turin ae.

66. Constable Massie's air is common in the Greig MSS. but is really only the second half of the tune; the whole tune is given under 'Harrowing Time' (70).

Drumdelgie

from Constable Massie.
4/06.

There' a fairmey up in Cairn - ey, That's kent baith far and wide to

rise in the mornin' ear - ly up - on sweet Deveron - side.

67. None of the three texts in the Greig MSS. has a recorded tune. This tune, from J. W. Spence, Rosecroft, Fyvie, is the only one given and has no accompanying words. It is a version of 'The Hills of Glenorchy'.

John Bruce o the Forenit

from J. W. Spence.

68. All the Greig tunes for 'Swaggers' are close variants of each other. The dotted rhythm in J. Mowat's tune is less pronounced than in the others.

Swaggers

from J. Mowat, Craigmaud, N.P.
9/07

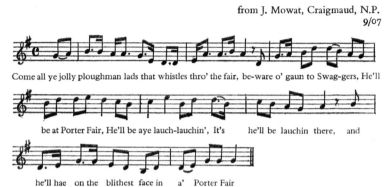

Come all ye jolly ploughman lads that whistles thro' the fair, be-ware o' gaun to Swag-gers, He'll

be at Porter Fair, He'll be aye lauch-lauchin', It's   he'll be lauchin there,   and

he'll hae on the blithest face in   a'   Porter Fair

69. The tune was recorded, like the text, from William Farquhar, Breakshill, Mintlaw.

Johnnie Sangster

from William Farquhar, Mintlaw.
1903

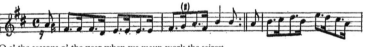

O a' the seasons o' the year when we maun work the sairest   We rise as seen as mornin' licht, nae
the harvest is the only time, and yet it is the rarest

craters can be blither, we buckle on oor finger steels and follow oot the scyther   For

you, Johnnie, you, Johnnie, You, Johnnie Sangster I'll trim the gavel o' my sheaf, For

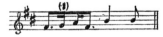

ye're the gallant bandster

218

70. As the two versions which supply both words and tunes have rather abbreviated texts, this ballad is represented by John Milne's text and George Ironside's tune. A note to Milne's text says the air is that of 'The Miller of Straloch', and since it is the same as that used for 'Drumdelgie', a 'Drumdelgie' version which is also marked for 'Harrowing Time' appears below. In Greig's experience, it was the most widely distributed of all folk-tunes. The MSS. show, however, that other tunes were also used for this song.

Harrowing Time

from Geo. Ironside
(by M. Milne) 11/08

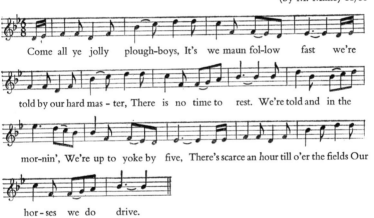

Come all ye jolly plough-boys, It's we maun fol-low fast we're told by our hard mas - ter, There is no time to rest. We're told and in the mor-nin', We're up to yoke by five, There's scarce an hour till o'er the fields Our hor-ses we do drive.

71. James Ewen's tune is fairly typical of the bothy ballad type that is Irish in origin or by imitation.

The Tarves Rant

from J. Ewen 8/06

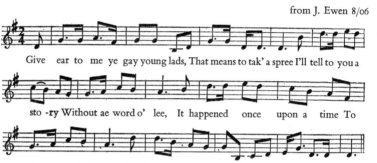

Give ear to me ye gay young lads, That means to tak' a spree I'll tell to you a

sto -ry Without ae word o' lee, It happened once upon a time To

Tarves we did go, To hae a spree and hae some fun, The truth I'll tell to you.

72. No tune is given in either the Greig or the Duncan MSS. for 'M'Ginty's Meal-an-Ale', but the composer wrote for Greig: 'Tune – "Roxburgh Castle", adapted (and ruined)'. 'Roxburgh Castle' is a well known English and Scottish hornpipe and country dance tune. The tune that was sung by Willie Kemp is printed in *Kerr's 'Cornkisters'* (Glasgow: Kerr, 1950), pp. 24-5.

Notes

5 [*Ch 35*] has a peculiar ambiguity in stanza 11; it would read more clearly if $10^{1,2}$ and $11^{3,4}$ were taken as one stanza and $10^{3,4}$ and $11^{1,2}$ as another. It would seem that Anna Brown was responding to the pull of the formulaic rhythms in both this story and 'The Laily Worm and the Machrel of the Sea' (*Ch 36*), where sister Maisry figures prominently; see especially 36: 2, 3.

6 [*Ch 37A*] has stanza 15 restored to the place it occupies in the manuscript.

7 and 8 [*Ch 53A and 53C*] are variants of the same story-theme, and are treated as separate narratives by Anna Brown.

9 [*Ch 62E*] provides a reference point for seeing, in fairly extreme form, the kind of localisation that can occur when a ballad-story moves from one culture area to another. One American version recorded in West Virginia in 1924 transplants the story to a frontier setting, with Annie initially captured by Indians and ransomed by the Lord Harry of a 'mansion-house' who fetches a bride from 'far over the river' because she brings him 'land and slaves' (Josiah H. Combs, *Folk-Songs of the Southern United States*, ed. D. K. Wilgus, Austin, 1967, pp. 114-18).

12 and 13 [*Ch 76D and 76E*] are two texts of the same ballad-story re-created seventeen years apart, the first in 1783, the second in 1800.

22 [*Ch 155A*] is a version of the legend that Chaucer also draws upon for 'The Prioress's Tale'.

23 [*Ch 203C*] seems to conflate separate incidents, of 1592 and 1666, in a Gordon-Farquharson feud. Mrs Brown, however, who was herself a Gordon and learned most of her ballads in Farquharson country, places the story in the seventeenth century:
the Baron of Braickly is a simple Narritive of a true story which happned as I have been told about the latter end of the 17 century. John Gordon of Braickly or as he was alwise call'd the Baron of Brackly w[ ]re man universally esteem'd he was of the Family of Aboyne & Farquharson of Inveray had a personal Ill will to him, & came with a train of armed followers & drove off his cattle. the Baron went out to remonstrate with him & was instantly sorrounded & cut to pieces not many yards from his own gate. Inveray fled & was outlaw'd but was allow'd afterwards to return I have been at Braickly & seen the ruins of the Barons castle little of which now remain they showd me the gates he rode out at about one half of which was then extant & a hollow way between two little knolls where the Farquharsons fell upon him – (letter of 18 June 1801 from Anna Brown to Robert Jamieson, in William Montgomerie, 'A

Bibliography of the Scottish Ballad Manuscripts 1730-1825: Part VII',
Studies in Scottish Literature, 7 [1970], 247-8).

28 [*Ch 41C*]   has only the magical mist left as vestige of the story's supernatural
elements; consequently, the emphasis on the 'gude kirking' is now dis-
proportionately heavy. 'Kirking' refers to the first church service attended,
particularly the first after an event such as a birth (as here) or wedding
or funeral.

29 [*Ch 65B*]   has enough of the transitional characteristics to supply a contrast
to Anna Brown's version (11). Consider, for example, the effect of
Nicol's stanza 15, which has no counterpart in *65A.*

33 [*Ch 173M*]   is based on events at the court of Mary, Queen of Scots,
although a similar event involving a Marie Hamilton occurred at a Czar's
court in the early eighteenth century.

34 [*Ch 188D*]   is a riding ballad of the Scottish Borders which attained a
certain currency in the Northeast, as it is also recorded by Peter Buchan,
by Gavin Greig from Bell Robertson, and in Michigan from an Aberdeen-
shire emigrant, John Laidlaw (see E. E. Gardner and G. J. Chickering,
Ballads and Songs of Southern Michigan, Ann Arbor, Michigan, 1939,
pp. 217-19).

35 [*Ch 196A*]   derives from an event in a local Gordon–Crichton feud of
1630.

36 [*Ch 198A*]   recounts an episode in the civil wars of the mid-seventeenth
century. John Seton was killed at the Bridge of Dee, just outside Aberdeen,
on 18 June 1639 when fighting for the royalist troops under Aboyne
against Montrose and the Covenanters. The disparaging stanzas about the
Highlanders, who were on the same side as Seton, refer to a skirmish a
few days previously when they had been thrown into confusion by
Montrose's cannon.

38 [*Ch 231D*]   is based on the domestic incompatibility of Sir Gilbert Hay,
tenth Earl of Erroll, and Lady Catherine Carnegie, younger daughter of
the second Earl of Southesk, who were married in 1658. He complains
that her father has not paid her tocher and she counters that, not being
'a sufficient man', he does not deserve the tocher. This allegation he dis-
proves, and they separate, the separation being recorded in some versions,
such as a Bell Robertson version, after this fashion:

> On Lady Errol's table
>   There stands clean dish an' speen,
> An' three times three it's cried o'er the gate,
>   'Lady Errol, come an' dine.'
>
> (*Last Leaves* B6)

40 'The Young Laird of Craigstoun' is one of the few ballads which by general agreement may be added to Child's collection. Many surviving texts are predominantly lyric but this one is narrative enough to warrant the story's inclusion. The text is from the Charles Kirkpatrick Sharpe transcript at Broughton House, Kirkcudbright, of the MS. entitled in the Scott transcript 'North Country Ballads'. A printed version of the Nicol text also appears in James Maidment, *A North Countrie Garland* (Edinburgh, 1824). The story is probably founded on the marriage of John Urquhart of Craigston to Elizabeth Innes and his early death in 1634. As Sharpe's text is untitled, this title comes from Maidment; other titles for the song are 'A-Growing', 'Still-A-Growing', and 'The Trees They Do Grow High'.

41 [*Ch 2*] represents one kind of riddling ballad, where the contest depends on the capping of impossibility with impossibility rather than the actual solving of riddles, as in 'Captain Wedderburn's Courtship'. This version is unusual in that it has the girl winning a husband through the contest instead of keeping an elfin knight at bay. The difference probably results from the tendency to rationalisation that characterises the later tradition.

45 [*Ch 24*] retains even in its fragmentary form the crucial motif of the story: that the ship will not sail for the captain because 'there's fey folk' aboard.

46 [*Ch 33*] is a broad burlesque of the loathly lady theme that occurs in 'The Marriage of Sir Gawain' [*Ch 31*] and 'King Henry' [*4; Ch 32*].

47 [*Ch 44*] is the merest fragment of a story that has a very long history. In the Scottish ballad the girl eludes her lover by a series of metamorphoses, all of which he counters until eventually, as in this climactic stanza, he masters her. The power of transformation was one of the powers attributed to the shamans, but appears in both shamanistic and heroic poetry. See C. M. Bowra, *Heroic Poetry* (London, 1952), p. 503, where he cites a Kara-Kirghiz poem in which the transformation-combat occurs in a heroic setting.

48 [*Ch 46*] is a text from the Greig MSS.

49 [*Ch 47*] is a fragmentary version of a ghost ballad where the revenant is called forth by the excessive pride of his sister.

50 [*Ch 58*] reinforces with its 'To Norowa, to Norowa' stanza the view advanced by Motherwell that the story recounts the fortunes of those who accompanied Margaret, daughter of Alexander III of Scotland, to Norway for her marriage with the Norwegian king, Eric.

51 [*Ch 138*] prints stanza 18 of this version for the first time. By mistake Greig inserted the additional stanza opposite another Bell Robertson ballad that appears a few pages earlier in the notebook.

52 [*Ch 170*]   concerns Jane Seymour, wife of Henry VIII, and the birth of Prince Edward. No trustworthy evidence substantiates the popularly held belief that she required extensive surgery at the birth.

53 and 54 [*Ch 178*]   are two, quite distinct, memorised versions of a ballad-story that deals with an event of 1571 in the long Gordon–Forbes feud. Sir Adam Gordon of Auchindoun, either in person or through the agency of his lieutenant, Captain Ker or Car, had the castle of Corgarff burned, causing the death of twenty-seven inhabitants, among them the chatelaine, Margaret Forbes of Towie.

56 [*Ch 237*]   is a text from the Greig MSS.

57 [*Ch 240*]   is a version of a ballad that changes its function in North America where, much reduced in scope, it becomes a lullaby.

61 [*Ch 274*]   is printed in the stanzaic order of Herd, as in *Last Leaves*, and not in the order received, namely: 7, 1, 8, 9, 10, 11, 12$^{1-4}$, 2, 3, 4, 5, 6, 12$^{5-8}$, 10a.

64   is a song that links the old and the new balladry in its joint emphasis on baronial milieu and ploughman's environment. Greig recorded this text from Mrs Sim, Rose Cottage, Hatton, Fintray.

65   merges in certain versions with 'Jock o' Rhynie' which in turn is related to 'In Praise of Huntly'. The generic nature of the experiences described fostered this kind of coalescence. The text was recorded from J. Mowat, Craigmaud, New Pitsligo.

66   was recorded from Constable Massie, Crimond.

67   was recorded from Annie Shirer, Kininmonth.

68   was recorded from J. Mowat, Craigmaud, New Pitsligo.

69   was recorded from William Farquhar, Breakshill, Mintlaw.

70   was recorded from John Milne, Maud.

71   was recorded from James Ewen, Loanhead, New Deer.

72   was recorded by Greig from the composer, George Bruce Thomson, New Deer.

Glossary

Where there exists only a minor difference in sound and spelling between the Scots and the English no gloss has been thought necessary; for example, flee/fly, fleer/floor, hame/home, lan/land, nane, neen/none, wa/wall, wi/with. In Northern Scots the initial 'wh' is pronounced 'f' as in fan/when, far, faur/where.

aboon, abeen *above*
ae *one, only*
ail *trouble, afflict*
an *and; if; one*
ashet *plate, dish*
aught (wha is—) *who owns*
ava *of all, at all*
ayock *a-yoke, at work*

baed *stopped*
bairn *child*
bale *harm, ill*
ban *hinge; band*
bandster *harvester who binds the sheaves*
bann *curse*
bannock *girdle-cake*
barley bree *whisky*
barn-well *'the well has no sense; and has probably been caught from 9, at the far well washing'* (Child)
beenie an' by *?; a corruption; in another Northeast text is 'Binyan's bay'*
beerly, bierly *great, portly*
ben *through the house*
bere *coarse barley*
bide *stay, wait; reside*
biggin *building, house*
bigly *commodious; handsomely wrought*
billy *comrade, brother*
bing *bin*
birk *birch*
birl *ply with drink*
blaket *blacked*

blawvin *blowing, playing*
blevet *corn bluebottle*
blinket *drunk*
body *person*
bore *crevice, hole*
borrow *release, ransom*
boun, boon *bound (for), ready to start*
bouted flowr *sifted flour*
bow (46: 3⁴) *pod*
bow (50: 8³) *boll, an old dry measure*
brain *mad*
brast *burst*
braw *handsome, handsomely dressed*
brecham *straw pack-saddle*
bree, broo *brow*
brigg *bridge*
brock *badger*
brod *pricking*
brookie *grimy, dirty*
brose *oatmeal dish, variously prepared*
bucht *(sheep-) pen*
burd, bird *maid*
burd-alone *by himself*
busk *make ready*
but, ben (8: 6¹, ² & 18: 2¹), butt *through the house*
but an, but than *and also*
byre *cattle shed*

ca *call; keep in motion; cart, transport*
caddie *young servant*
camowine *camomile*
cannie *cautious, careful;* (69: 7⁷) *pleasant, (?) lucky*
carket *necklace*

carle *fellow, peasant*
carline *old woman*
caul *cold*
chap *knock*
chapper (tatie —) *potato masher*
chess *strap, jess*
chiel *man*
claw *scratch*; (65: 7⁴) *strike out with*
clockin *broody*
clootit *patched*
close *courtyard; farmyard*
cod *pillow*
coffer *box, chest*
compass *circle*
cordwain *Cordovan leather*
corn *feed with oats*
couth *sound, word*
cowe *twig*
crater *creature*
creesh *grease*
crouselie *proudly*
cumbruk *cambric*

dabble *soak and disarrange*
daigh *dough*
danting (38: cho.) *sexual play*
dee *die; do*
ding, *pa. p.* dang *fall heavily and continuously*
do to (with reflexive pronoun) *betake*
dochter, dother *daughter*
doited *in a state of dotage*
dokin *dock plant, something of little value*
doole *sorrow, grief*
doot *doubt*
douce *sedate, quiet*
dowie *sad, doleful*
dree *suffer, endure*
dreepin *dripping*
dung *struck*
dyke *wall*

eely pig *oil jar*
een, eyne *eyes*

een *one*
eident *steady*
eneuch *enough*

fa *fall; who*
fae, *prep., n.* *from; foe*
fairlie *marvel, wonder*
fame, faem *ocean, (river-) water*
faul *fold*
fee, *v.* *engage as servant, esp. for half-yearly*
feel *fool*
Feersday *Thursday*
fess *fetch*
fey *destined to die*
finger-steel *finger-stall*
firlot *an old dry measure*
flaffin *frivolous*
fleerishin *steel for lighting fire with flint*
flude *flood*
foo *how*
foreby *nearby*
forlorn *lost*
forn *cared for* (pa. p. *fare*)
fou *full; drunk*
fushion (without —) *physically weak*

gab *beak, mouth*
gae *go; gave*
gaed, ged, gid *went*
gains for me *suits my need*
gaire, gare *triangular piece of cloth inserted in a garment; gusset*
gang, gyang *go*
gantrees *barrel-stands*
gar *make*
garl *? gravel*
gavel *a bundle of cut corn before it is bound into a sheaf*
gavellock *iron crowbar*
gaw *gall*
gear *goods*
gey (71: 5⁶) *fine* (ironic)
gimp *neat, slender*

gin *if*

gin (34: 6²) *apparatus for securing a door*

girn *grumble*

glaned *glanced, shone*

glee *glove*

gleed *fire*

gollach *insect*

goons *gowns*

goud, gowd *gold*

gowany *daisy-covered*

graith *equipment (horse and arms)*

greet *weep*

greetin fou *maudlin drunk*

grippet *constricted*

groom, greeme *young man, fellow*

grumphy *pig*

gryte *great*

gueede, guide, gweed *good*

gurious *grim, grisly*

gyaun *going*

hack *crack in the skin*

had, haud *hold*

hailing *falling fast*

haind grass *kept for hay, preserved from pasturing*

hairst *harvest, autumn*

hap *cover*

harl *roughcast*

harrit *harrowed*

hause-bane *neck-bone*

heelster-gowdy *head over heels*

heely *slowly, gently*

heowe (green —) *greenish*

hielan, heelan *highland*

high-colld *'high-cut', made to go to the knee or above*

hight *was called*

hinches *haunches*

hint *instant*

hireman *hired servant, farm labourer*

hissy-skip *housewife's work-basket*

howe *hollow, dale*

hunt's ha *hunting lodge*

hyne *away, hence*

ilka; ilkane *each, every; each one*

ire (thro —) (20: 17⁴) *'through ither'; i.e., the parts burned through one another*

jaw *wave*

jelly hind greeme *handsome young man*

jockey coat *greatcoat*

kail *borecole; cabbage; vegetable soup*

kaim, kemb, kame *comb*

keegerin *puddling*

keist the cavils *cast lots*

ken *know*

kep, keep *catch*

(a') kin kind *all sorts*

kirking *ceremonial kirk attendance for, e.g the first time after a wedding, birth, or funeral*

kirn *wallow*

kist *chest*

kitchie-nook *kitchen- (chimney-) corner*

knave-bairn *boy, male child*

knowe *hillock, knoll*

kye *cattle*

lad-bairn *boy*

laigh-colld *low-cut*

lair *learning*

lamer *amber*

langsome *wearily long*

laudamy *laudanum*

laverock *lark*

lax *relief*

lead *gen. carry or cart; specif. carry harvested grain or hay from the field to the stackyard*

leaf *luff, loof, as opposed to lee, the weather-side*

lemman, leman *lover, mistress*

leuch, leugh, lauch *laugh*

leve *remainder*
Leve (58: 3³) *lovely, pleasant*
leven *grassy ground*
lillie (6: 12²) *lovely, charming*
limmer *malevolent woman*
lingcan *body*
lockerin *curling*
loof *palm*
loon, loun *boy*
loose *louse*
loup, lap *jump, jumped*
lout, loot *bend down, bow*
lowse *unyoke, untie; loose*
lugs (owre the — wi) *completely given over to*

mak to (66: 5³) *make wisps from the straw passing out of a threshing mill*
make, maick *mate*
mane, maun, *must*
mary *maid (of honour)*
mat *may*
mavis *thrush*
meal, *v. thicken (soup) by adding meal; feed*
meal-an'-ale *harvest home celebration*
meare, meer *mare*
meed *mood; reward*
mell *wooden hammer*
men (11: 28⁴) *make amends*
mess *measure out portions*
mickel, muckle *much, great*
mild *meek, demure*
millering *waste meal*
mind (on) *remember*
mold *ground*
muskadine *muscatel*

naughtless *good-for-naught, impotent*
neep *turnip*
neiper, neebor *neighbour*
neist *next*
nickum *rogue*
niffer *exchange*

not *needed*
nourice, neerice *nurse*

or *before*
orra (68: 13³) *extra, beyond the ordinary*

pa, pall *fine cloth*
parkit *put out to pasture in a field*
peel *scrape the skin off*
peetyfu *pitiful*
philabeg *kilt*
piece *snack*
pig *jar*
pine, *n., v. pain; waste away*
pints *laces*
pit (66: 10⁴) *help move*
piz-meal *peasemeal*
plack *small Scots coin*
plough *an area of land*
poke *sack, bag*
pree (— her mou) *kiss, 'sample'*
pudden-bree *liquid in which the puddings are boiled*
pun *pound*
puttin-stane *stone impelled from the shoulder in athletic competition*

quarter *measure of grain*
queet *ankle*
querren stane *hand-mill; quinie-stane (cornerstone) makes better sense*

rabble rook *riotous company*
rae *roe (-deer)*
raip *rope; rope of straw or hay made on the farm*
rake *move hurriedly*
ranting *roistering, romping, revelling*
rauked *raked, searched*
redd *tidy, clean up*
reef-tree *roof-tree, beam in the angle of a roof*
reek *smoke*
reel *be boisterous*
reese *boast, praise*

rickle *clatter down*

rig *raised strip of ploughed land*

rive *tear*

roddins *berries of the rowan or mountain ash*

room ye roun *make room by moving round*

roost *rust*

roset *resin*

rottons *rats*

routh *plenty*

row *wrap*

ruckie *dim. of ruck, a stack of hay or corn*

rug *pull, tug*

rung *ring, noise*

sair *sore, sorely*

sair *serve*

sal *shall*

sark *shirt*

sat *salt*

sautie *salty*

scaud *scold*

scuttle-dishes *serving dishes*

seely (court) *fairy*

set *suit, befit*

shalt *small pony*

sheave *slice*

shed *a stretch of crop-bearing ground*

shed by *drew back from his face*

sheen, shoon *shoes*

shortsome *divert*

showr *pain*

sicken, sick *such*

side *long*

siller, sillert *silver*

skeel *skill*

sklaitit *slated*

skyelf *shelf*

skyrl *shriek, cry or sing shrilly*

slack *narrow pass or bog*

slae *sloe*

sneed *hairband, ribbon, snood*

snell *bitingly cold, keen*

snod *trim, secure*

soladene *greater celandine*

sort *look after, clean up*

soss *mess*

souter *shoemaker*

sowens *a dish made from oats*

spaul *animal's shoulder*

speer, spear *ask*

spurtle *stirring-rod*

sta *stole; stall*

stap, stappit *step, stepped*

stap *cram*

stark *strong*

steer *robust*

steer *confusion*

stickit *killed*

stock *the outer side of a box-bed*

stook *put into stooks or shocks*

stoot *well-built, strong, stout*

stot *young bull*

stoup *bucket*

strae, stray *straw*

strait *tighten*

straucht *straight; make straight*

streen (the —) *last night, yestreen*

sue *sew*

suthron *southernwood*

syne *then*

tae, tane . . . tither *the one . . . the other*

tang *piece of unwrought iron*

tapetan *not known*

tappit *crested*

taul *told*

tet, tett *lock of hair*

teuchit *lapwing, peewit*

thack *thatching*

theek *thatch, line*

theets *traces*

think lang *grow weary*

thole *suffer patiently, endure*

thraw *twist*

tide *time*
timmer *wood*
tine *lose*
tinkie *tinker*
tirl at the pin *rattle at door-fastening or early form of knocker*
tocher *dowry*
toors *towers*
toun, toon *hamlet; farm*
tour (lyin in a —) *straight route*
trapand *treacherously dealt with*
tree *pole, shaft*
tricle *treacle*
troch *trough*
trow (I —) *I can assure you*
true, trow *believe, trust*
tryst *entice*
twal *twelve*
twalmonth *twelve-month, year*
twin *separate*
tyawvin *wrestling, horseplay*

unco, *adj.*, *adv.* *uncommon, extraordinary; very*
unseily *unhappy, unlucky*
unthought lang *(keep from) wearying*
usher oot *issue forth*

wad, wid *would*
wad (58: 6^1) *wager*
wain *dwelling-place, here cage*
wallwood *wild-wood*

wally *sorrow*
wan *dark-coloured; colourless*
wan (55: 10^2) *direction, area*
wan'ert *wandered*
war, waur *worse*
wardles make *worldly mate; earthly consort*
ware *use*
waught *draught*
weal, weel *welfare*
wedder *wether*
weed *clothing*
weety *rainy*
well-fard, weel-faurd *well-favoured, pretty, handsome*
whin *furze*
white money *silver*
wide *wade*
wierd *lot, destiny*
wight *strong, lively*
wile *vile*
win, won, in, up *get in, up*
won *dwell*
wrack (in a —) *broken down*
wyle *lure*
wyte (I —) *I assure you*

yate, yett *gate*
yeard-fast *fixed firmly in the earth*
yirnin *whining*
yoke *begin; set to; yoke*
yokin *itching*

Index

Allison Gross   23, 221
Archie o Cawfield   120, 222

Barnyards o' Delgaty, The   191, 216, 224
Baron of Brackley, The   82, 221
Bonnie Annie   146, 223
Bonny Baby Livingston   83
Bonny John Seton   125, 222
Brown Robin   62, 212

Captain Wedderburn's Courtship   148, 223
Child Waters   36
Clerk's Twa Sons o Owsenford, The   109

Death of Queen Jane, The   156, 224
Drumdelgie   192, 217, 224
Duke of Gordon's Daughter, The   161, 224

Earl of Errol, The   129, 222
Edom o Gordon   157, 158, 224
Elfin Knight, The   137, 223
Eppie Morrie   127

Fair Annie   33, 221
Fair Mary of Wallington   55
Fause Foodrage   51
Fire of Frendraught, The   122, 222

Gardener, The   159
Gay Goshawk, The   59, 211
Get Up and Bar the Door   180
Gil Brenton   11, 207

Harrowing Time   200, 219, 224
Hind Etin   101, 222
Hind Horn   143
Hireman Chiel, The   185, 216, 224

John Bruce o the Forenit   194, 217, 224
Johnie Scot   65, 213
Johnnie Sangster   198, 218, 224

Kemp Owyne   95
Kempy Kay   146, 223
King Henry   20, 210
Kitchie-Boy, The   88
Knight and Shepherd's Daughter, The   111

Lady Isabel and the Elf-Knight   138
Lady Maisry   40, 102, 211, 222
Lamkin   56
Lang Johnny More   169
Lass of Roch Royal, The   44, 47, 221
Leesome Brand   140
Lord Ingram and Chiel Wyet   106
Love Gregor   47, 221

Mary Hamilton   118, 222
M'Ginty's Meal-an-Ale   204, 220, 224

Our Goodman   177, 224

Proud Lady Margaret   151, 223

Rantin Laddie, The   165, 224
Robin Hood and Allen a Dale   154, 223
Rose the Red and White Lily   73, 215

Sir Hugh   80, 221
Sir Patrick Spens   152, 223
Swaggers   196, 218, 224

Tam Lin   97
Tarves Rant, The   202, 219, 224
Thomas Rymer   24, 221
Twa Magicians, The   147, 223

Twa Sisters, The   18, 209

White Fisher, The   174
Wife Wrapt in Wether's Skin, The
   181
Willie o Douglas Dale   69, 214
Willie's Lady   15, 208

Young Allan   166
Young Bearwell   131
Young Bekie   29, 210, 221
Young Bicham   26, 221
Young Laird of Craigstoun, The
   133, 223